PAPER CRAFTS

A MAKER'S GUIDE

PAPER CRAFTS

A MAKER'S GUIDE

With over 220 photographs and illustrations

First published in the United Kingdom in 2018
by Thames & Hudson Ltd in association with the
Victoria and Albert Museum, London

Paper Crafts: A Maker's Guide
© 2018 Victoria and Albert Museum, London/
Thames & Hudson Ltd, London

V&A images © 2018 Victoria and Albert Museum, London
Illustrations and project photography © 2018
Thames & Hudson Ltd, London
Text and layout © 2018 Thames & Hudson Ltd, London

See also Picture Credits p.176

Design by Hyperkit
Illustrations by Eleanor Crow
Projects commissioned by Amy Christian
Project editing by Faye Robson
Project photography by We Are Studio

British Library Cataloguing-in-Publication Data
A catalogue record for this book is available from
the British Library

ISBN 978-0-500-29418-5

Printed and bound in China by Toppan Leefung
Printing Limited

To find out about all our publications, please visit
www.thamesandhudson.com. There you can subscribe
to our e-newsletter, browse or download our current
catalogue, and buy any titles that are in print.

Frontispiece: Anna Maria Garthwaite, papercut, 1707,
Great Britain
Knife-cut cut-paper work, with pin pricking and collage,
paper and ink on a vellum backing
V&A: E.1077-1993

Back cover images (clockwise, from top left):
Papercut (detail), 1986, depicting symbols of abundance,
Fengning, China, 9.5 x 15 cm (3¾ x 6 in.)
V&A: FE.143-1992

Lee Young Soon, three woven paper jars (detail), 2009–12
Hanji, jiseung technique, South Korea, height x widest
point: 35 x 31 cm (13¾ x 12 in.); 32 x 24 cm (12½ x 9½ in.);
26 x 25 cm (10¼ x 10 in.)
V&A: FE.78-80–2015. Purchase funded by Samsung

Teleorama no. 1 (detail), *c.* 1825
Hand-coloured etchings on paper, cardboard and
paper bellows, front panel: 11.8 x 14.5 cm (4¾ x 5¾ in.),
length: approx. 66 cm (26 in.; extended)
National Art Library, V&A: Gestetner 1

Laura Muir Mackenzie. Unknown Family Group (detail)
Cut paper, Scotland, 15 x 20 cm (6 x 8 in.)
V&A: P.58–1930.

Mask, 1972, Varanasi, India
Papier mâché, 29.5 x 30 cm (11½ x 12 in.)
V&A: IS.10–1977

Peter Murdoch/Perspective Designs Ltd, 'Chair Thing',
1968, Great Britain
Laminated paper, 49 x 44 x 36 cm (19¼ x 17¼ x 14 in.)
V&A: CIRC.795-1968. Given by the Council
of Industrial Design

V&A Publishing
Supporting the world's leading
museum of art and design,
the Victoria and Albert
Museum, London

PAPER CRAFTS TODAY

Rob Ryan is a London-based artist working primarily in the medium of papercutting. His output, often consisting of whimsical figures paired with sentimental, grave, honest and occasionally humorous text, has resulted in collaborations with brands ranging from _Vogue_ to Liberty of London and Tatty Devine.

When you were young you still believed in magic, but then you reached an age when you stopped. But, years later, you began to realize that there are countless, seemingly normal things that exist all around us that really are more magical than any fantasy.

I always thought that the wonderful thing about art was how, using so little, you could make so much. Henri Matisse, with a humble pencil, might use up only a fraction of a millimetre of its lead in producing something, in just a few dozen strokes, that perfectly captured the very essence of grace and beauty. What this meant to me was that there was never an excuse not to create – at least not for want of materials. I was not having it. A few basic things – some paper, a pencil, paint, water, oil – were the only ingredients (beside your imagination) that you needed to make a magical thing that could enter someone's mind and start to change their perception of the world.

But for some artworks, it might be enough to have just one material. Creativity is not only about having to make and build, but also about having to change and destroy. What else did Michelangelo do to create a masterpiece except take a solid block of marble and remove just enough until his David appeared?

I was drawn to working in paper because I liked the limitations it imposed on me. I never quite knew when a painting was supposed to be finished and I always proceeded to add more and more layers of paint, long after the work's best moment had passed. Working on cutting a picture out of a single piece of paper eliminated this problem, because there would always be a point when there was no more paper left to cut out. More planning was involved; the end was always a part of the beginning.

Papercutting for me is really as much about drawing as cutting: I don't make a single cut on the paper until the entire piece is drawn out. People often ask me how long it takes to cut out a piece of work but the cutting is really immaterial – all the real work is done with a pencil. All the planning and sketching and rubbing out and redrawing is the hard work, and the papercutting is the final part, which gives the space between my lines a solid body and finally brings the whole to life.

This book presents ways of working with paper that are 2D as well as sculptural, and techniques as varied as knotting, twisting, folding, braiding, quilling and cutting. I think that people who like to work with paper in all these different ways are drawn to the limitations and difficulties that the medium so often presents; they don't see obstacles, but challenges to be overcome through their own wit and creativity. The variety of ways in which paper can be shaped are also testament to its fundamental versatility as a medium.

The American artist Kara Walker (see p.8) references the historical tradition of papercut silhouettes – popular among the genteel classes of the eighteenth and early nineteenth centuries – in powerful artworks and installations that expose historical abuses and hypocrisy. The Philadelphia-based artist Lydia Ricci (see p.9) makes tiny models of trucks and books and pinball machines out of scraps of old card and printed bits of paper – the ephemera that fill our allotted years go on to form these models of the everyday objects we share our lives with. For some reason, her work is both reassuring and heartbreaking at the same time. Meanwhile, in London, you feel as if the illustrator Chrissie Macdonald (see p.9) could turn her hand to re-making the whole world in paper if she put her mind to it; her ingenuity seems limitless and as she bends and folds paper and card, you forget that paper is a fragile, easily torn material. It becomes a credible replacement for the real thing: the illusion is complete.

To work with a material so light, so delicate and yet surprisingly strong requires a temperament (and fingers) equally as flexible, resilient and multi-talented as paper itself. I invite all makers to experiment with the projects presented here and discover some of these qualities and capacities within themselves.

Rob Ryan, *Ladder Kiss*, 2006
Hand-cut paper

Rob Ryan, *Give Me Work*, 2012
Hand-cut paper

Kazue Honma, *Mobius sculpture*, 2004, Japan
Strapping tape and persimmon tannin,
18 x 28 x 31 cm (7 x 11 x 12 in.)
V&A: FE.14-2004

Richard Sweeney, *Untitled*, 2013
Paper, monofilament nylon, lead
Installation for Miniartextil exhibition,
Montrouge, Paris, 2013

Kara Walker, *Darkytown
Rebellion*, 2001
(installation view:
American Primitive,
Brent Sikkema, New York
Cut paper and projection
on wall, approx.
4.5 x 100 m (15 x 33 ft)

Lydia Ricci, *Call Waiting*, 2016

Robert Ebendorf, neckpiece, 1985, USA
Japanese rice paper, 24-carat gold
leaf, lacquer, oxidized silver, copper
and ebony, diameter: 28.5 cm (11 in.)
V&A: M.5-1989. Given by Tom Weisz

Diane Meyersohn, paper dress, 1967,
Great Britain
Bonded cellulose fibre ('Bondina') with
printed design, length: 81.5 cm (32 in.)
V&A: T.176-1986. Given by Diane Meyersohn

Chrissie Macdonald, *Paper Shredder*, 2009

TOOLS & MATERIALS

In this section we outline the essential tools and materials typically used in paper crafts, many of which you may already have at home. These items can all be found at arts and crafts suppliers and online. The specific tools and materials you will need are listed at the beginning of each of the projects in the book.

Paper

Paper is a popular material for arts and crafts because of its affordability and tactility. It comes in many different colours, weights and textures and lends itself to a wide range of techniques.

Choosing the right paper

Internationally, paper is measured in grams per square metre (gsm) and, in America, in pounds per ream, with a ream typically running to 500 sheets of paper. We have grouped papers into three broad weight categories below, to give you an idea of the best uses for each, although recommended paper weights are also listed at the start of each project. Experiment with different papers to find what works best for you.

Lightweight paper: We would classify lightweight paper as anything below 120 gsm – ideal for folding, shaping, intricate papercuts and for practising other techniques. Lightweight paper can be cut effortlessly with a scalpel or scissors.

Mid-weight paper: Paper weighing between 120 and 200 gsm is great for all kinds of paper crafts, and can be cut quite easily with a scalpel or scissors (5 & 6).

Heavyweight paper: Paper weighing over 200 gsm, making it ideal for adding structure. This kind of paper may require a heavy-duty knife or scissors to cut cleanly and stronger glues to hold it in position.

As well as different weights, paper comes in a range of textures and finishes:

Uncoated paper: As its name suggests, uncoated paper has no extra coating or paper finishing and tends to be rougher and more textured than coated paper. It is commonly used in paper crafts for this reason.

Coated paper: This paper comes in a range of finishes, with the most popular coatings being gloss, matt and silk (somewhere between matt and gloss). Coated paper is generally very smooth and is more resistant to dirt, moisture and wear.

Embossed paper: Papers with embossing have textures and patterns pressed into their surfaces. They are generally uncoated and have a highly tactile, premium aesthetic.

Popular paper types

As a general rule, try to use good-quality, acid-free or pH-neutral paper, as it cuts cleanly and does not fade over time, giving your work a longer shelf life. Alternatively, you can also recycle existing paper products for your own paper craft projects; you may have old maps, encyclopedias, books, newspapers and magazines at home, all of which are a great source of paper for decorative projects. You can even use banknotes (see pp.34–39). Specialist craft papers are also available, often sold in themed selections, and cut to a standard size (see pp.28–31).

Paper yarn: This can be found in many craft stores and online (1). It is often used in giftwrapping but can also be used for weaving (see pp.164–69).

Tissue paper: A lightweight, translucent paper, available in many colours, often sold in large sheets (2).

Recycled paper: This sort of paper typically has lots of short fibres and is not recommended for papercutting, as it is likely to tear (3).

Newsprint: A thin, low-cost paper stock (4) used most commonly in papier mâché and découpage projects (see pp.150–53, 106–9).

Tracing paper: A lightweight, crisp, translucent paper (7). Essential for transferring designs and templates (see p.19).

Unryu or 'Dragon' paper: A strong, lightweight, acid-free paper with a swirling texture, used in origami (see pp.34–45) and other forms of paper crafting (8).

Crepe paper: A form of tissue paper treated to create tiny gathers over the surface – great for sculpting and commonly used in making paper flowers. Crepe paper is also available in a double-sided variant often known as doublette, which has a different colour on each side.

Découpage paper: This paper comes in a variety of weights and finishes and is typically patterned and printed, ready to be cut out (see pp.106–9). Print-at-home découpage designs are also available online.

Card stock: A generic term for paper weighing over 130 gsm (9). Card stock comes in many different textures, colours and weights and is both widely available and inexpensive.

Foam board/foam core: A strong and lightweight material made from polystyrene coated in paper. It is easily cut with a sharp craft knife and can be used to add structure and as a mount or backing in picture frames.

Quilling paper: This paper comes in thin strips of varying widths, though you can make your own by trimming sheets of paper using a guillotine or scalpel and metal ruler (see photograph on p.99).

Washi paper: A luxurious, handmade paper that originated in Japan. Washi paper has long fibres and an uneven surface. It is stronger than many paper types and is great to use for origami projects.

Standard paper sizes

The international paper size standard is ISO 216, in which the ratio between width and height is always the square root of 2. In North America, a different system is used, with the most common paper sizes being Letter (8½ x 11 in.), Legal (8½ x 14 in.) and Ledger/Tabloid (11 x 17 in.). These are indicated below on the A Series chart in dotted lines.

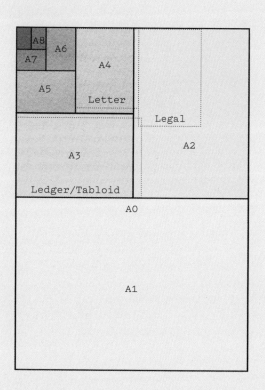

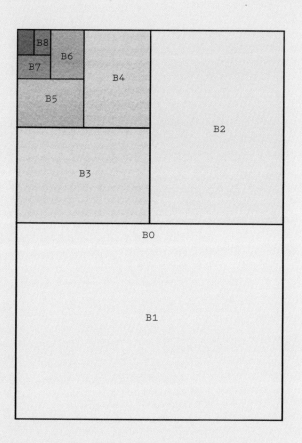

A Series

A	Width x Height (mm)	Width x Height (in.)
A0	841 x 1,189	33.1 x 46.8
A1	594 x 841	23.4 x 33.1
A2	420 x 594	16.5 x 23.4
A3	297 x 420	11.7 x 16.5
A4	210 x 297	8.3 x 11.7
A5	148 x 210	5.8 x 8.3
A6	105 x 148	4.1 x 5.8
A7	74 x 105	2.9 x 4.1
A8	52 x 74	2.0 x 2.9
A9	37 x 52	1.5 x 2.0
A10	26 x 37	1.0 x 1.5

B Series

B	Width x Height (mm)	Width x Height (in.)
B0	1,000 x 1,414	39.4 x 55.7
B1	707 x 1,000	27.8 x 39.4
B2	500 x 707	19.7 x 27.8
B3	353 x 500	13.9 x 19.7
B4	250 x 353	9.8 x 13.9
B5	176 x 250	6.9 x 9.8
B6	125 x 176	4.9 x 6.9
B7	88 x 125	3.5 x 4.9
B8	62 x 88	2.4 x 3.5
B9	44 x 62	1.7 x 2.4
B10	31 x 44	1.2 x 1.7

Wrapping paper: Available in many colours, weights and finishes, wrapping paper is an easy way to add colour and texture to a project (10).

Origami paper: Thin paper that is specifically designed to be easy to fold cleanly (11). It tends to be patterned or coloured on one side and plain on the other.

Printer or copier paper: A staple in many homes, printer paper is typically 80 gsm (see p.11) and is great for sketching out designs or practising compositions before committing to your chosen paper, though, with its crisp, matt surface, it also makes a useful crafting material in its own right.

Grey board: A heavyweight, 100% recycled, pulp-fibre cardboard used to add structure to craft projects.

Paper grain

Like wood, most paper has a grain – the direction in which long fibres of the paper are aligned, parallel to one another. Most paper will be more flexible in one direction, 'with the grain' (parallel to the grain direction), than in the other ('against the grain'). To find the grain of your paper, gently flex it in one direction, then rotate it 90 degrees and flex it again. It should flex more easily in one direction. Paper will also tear more easily in the grain direction. Grain is important and makes a difference to how a paper will react when you use it.

Bookbinding: Book covers and pages should have the grain running parallel to the spine. If the grain runs in the wrong direction, the pages will be difficult to turn and the cover may warp and buckle. A similar principle applies when folding cards: the fold should made be parallel to the grain so that paper fibres are not broken.

Flower making (see pp.156–61): When using crepe paper, the grain is especially important. This paper can be sculpted and manipulated when shaping against the grain.

Gluing: When attaching two pieces of paper, try to ensure that the grain of both runs in the same direction. When applying glue, moisture is introduced to paper, causing it to swell and sometimes buckle (more so in the grain direction). Consistent grain direction will reduce this and help to prevent your two sheets pulling apart.

Quilling or curling (see pp.96–103): When cutting quilling strips, cut against the grain, making the cut fibres shorter and easier to curl.

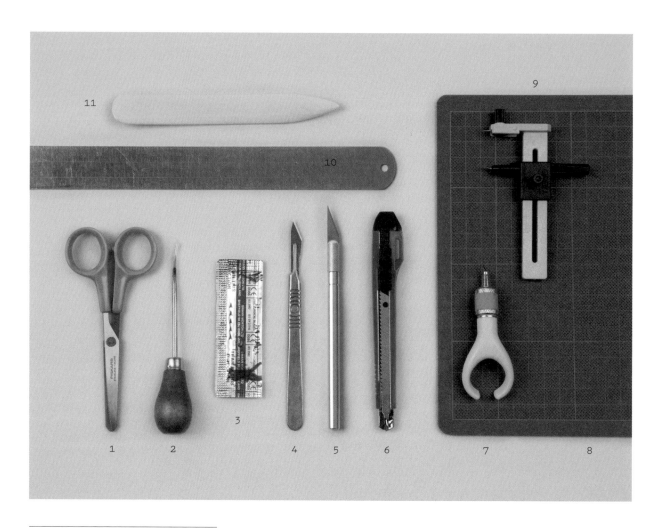

Cutting tools

The decision of which cutting tool to use often comes down to personal preference, with comfort, safety and function playing important roles.

Guillotine or paper trimmer
A larger tool designed to effortlessly cut paper along a straight edge.

Craft scissors (1)
Should be sharp and sit comfortably in your hand. Embroidery scissors are great for intricate cutting. For heavier paper you may require a larger pair.

Awl (2)
A small, pointed tool used for piercing holes, even in heavier materials such as card or even leather (in bookbinding).

Surgical scalpels (4)
A scalpel usually has a flat metal handle and holds a thin and flexible surgical blade (3). See opposite for some useful blades.

Craft knives (5)
These hold thicker, rigid blades and often have round handles and textured grips. A knurled collar or collet secures the blade in place.

Retractable knives or box cutters (6)
This sort of heavy-duty knife is great for cutting straight lines and for use with thicker materials such as cardboard and heavyweight paper.

Circle cutter (9)
A useful tool, used to effortlessly and accurately cut circular apertures.

Swivel knife (7)
This fits onto your finger and allows greater accuracy when cutting intricate shapes and curved lines.

Cutting mat (8)
A self-healing cutting mat is essential for most paper crafts projects. They come in all shapes, sizes and colours and will protect your work surface from sharp blades. One with a ruled grid will help you measure and line up edges when cutting.

Metal ruler (10)
Another paper-crafting essential, used for cutting straight lines and scoring. Never use a plastic or wooden ruler with a scalpel or blade. Choose one that measures in both metric and imperial for precision in your crafting.

Knife safety

It is important to handle sharp blades carefully to avoid injury.

Safe use of blades

1. Keep your hand and the rest of your body away from the cutting line.

2. Work on a stable, uncluttered surface, protected by a cutting mat.

3. Only use your knife or scissors for their intended purpose, not in place of a scraper, screwdriver or chisel.

4. Use a metal ruler when cutting straight lines. Plastic and wooden rulers are likely to slip.

5. Do not attempt to catch a dropped pair of scissors or knife.

6. Don't press too hard when using knives and blades.

7. When using scissors, cut in a direction away from your body.

8. Always pass a pair of scissors handle first to another person.

Attaching a surgical blade

Use the following procedure to safely attach blades to handles with a bayonet fitting:

1. Grip the blade with pliers or similar, avoiding contact with the cutting edge.

2. Place the blade part-way over the handle fitting and engage slots. Slide the blade until it clicks into position.

Removing a surgical blade

You can purchase blade removers or use the following procedure to remove a blade with a bayonet fitting:

1. Grip the blade with your pliers, making sure that the cutting edge is turned away from the hand and body.

2. Ensure the blade is pointing downwards. While holding the handle firmly, lift the back edge of the blade with the pliers and slide away the handle.

Attaching and removing an ACM blade

Use the following procedure to safely attach blades to craft handles that have a knurled collar or collet fitting.

1. Rotate the collar anti-clockwise to loosen the collet.

2. Insert the blade and rotate the collar clockwise to secure the blade and lock it in place.

3. Remove the blade by rotating the collar anti-clockwise until the collet has loosened its grip, then carefully slide out the blade.

Disposing of blades

Never throw used blades in a domestic bin. Invest in a sharps box in which to keep your used blades, then, once it is full, investigate your local safe disposal point.

Some useful blades

11, ACM (Arts, Crafts & Modellers)
This type of blade is very sturdy, with a sharp point. ACM blades are not recommended for fine details, as they are very rigid and much thicker than surgical blades. Perfect for cutting straight lines, simple shapes and thicker materials.

10a, Surgical
A popular, curved blade with a sharp point, which offers flexibility when cutting curves and intricate shapes.

11, Surgical
A popular blade among papercutters, the 11 blade is long and flexible, which helps when cutting curves and intricate shapes.

15a, Surgical
A short blade perfect for small details; the shorter length means limited flexibility but increases control.

Swivel
As the name suggests, swivel blades are perfect for cutting curves in a single smooth motion, as compared with fixed blades, which require you to move the paper to continue with a curve. This type of blade can usually only be used with a handle of the same brand for which it was specifically designed.

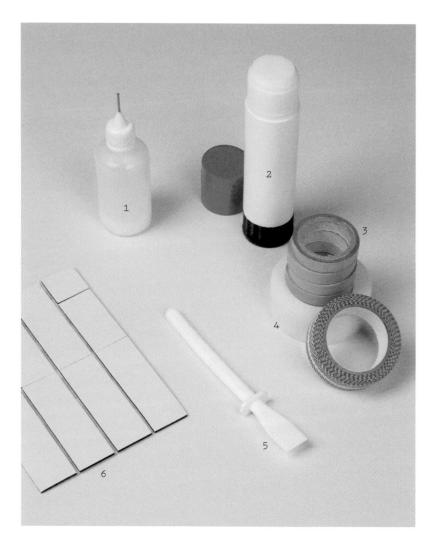

Double-sided foam pads (6)
Coated with adhesive on both sides, these are perfect for layering and adding depth to compositions.

All-purpose adhesive
A clear, repositionable glue that dries quickly. Great for paper crafts as it does not cause paper to wrinkle.

Spray mount
Repositionable spray adhesive, which allows you to make adjustments to a paper layout.

Hot-melt glue gun
Ideal for a wide range of craft projects. Clear glue sticks are melted in the gun and the resulting glue squeezed through a nozzle. Sets quickly, for a strong, permanent hold.

Safe use of glues and solvents

Glues and solvents may be toxic, so treat them carefully.

1. Spray adhesives discharge fine particles and some adhesives and varnishes may also have toxic elements. Only use spray adhesives in large, ventilated areas or outdoors.

2. Store your varnishes and adhesives in a cool, dry place, out of reach of children.

3. When using spray adhesive, it is recommended that you protect your hands and eyes with gloves and safety goggles. You may also want to use a facemask to avoid inhaling fumes.

Tapes, glues and adhesives

PVA or white glue (1)
PVA (polyvinyl alcohol) is a water-based (and therefore easily washable) glue that dries clear, though it is best used sparingly as it tends to warp or wrinkle paper. PVA can also be layered and used as a varnish. Use with a glue spreader (5) for conisistent coverage.

Glue stick (2)
Can be used to quickly stick surfaces together with minimum mess.

Washi tape (3)
Low-tack, decorative masking tape that comes in different colours and patterns. Great for decoration or for temporary applications. Often used for gift wrapping but also available in craft stores.

'Magic' tape (4)
The matt finish of this tape is almost invisible when stuck to paper, so is useful for fixing mistakes.

Masking tape
Low-tack, paper-based tape, useful for protecting paper and for temporary sticking or positioning.

Double-sided tape
Coated with adhesive on both sides and used to invisibly and permanently stick two surfaces together.

Useful extras and specialist tools

Some paper crafts require specialist items (although alternatives can often be found in the home). The equipment needed for each project is listed on the introductory page under 'You will need'.

Bone folder (11 – p.14)

Traditionally made from bone, as its name suggests, but now more commonly from plastic. This tool is used to create smooth creases and folds without cracking paper.

Stationery

An HB pencil, mechanical pencil and/or marker pen are useful to have on hand for any paper crafts project. Coloured pens can be used to decorate finished pieces, as can inks and paints. A good eraser is an essential, and a hole punch and paperclips are useful for securing paper in place.

Rubber stamps

Used with ink pads, rubber stamps are available to buy in many designs, and are a quick and easy way of printing onto paper. You can also make your own rubber stamps very easily by carving a design into an eraser with a craft knife.

Varnish

Quick-drying, matt, clear wood varnish is recommended for découpage projects (see pp.106–9). Applying multiple layers of varnish to a decorated surface will make it more hardwearing.

Dried flowers

Add natural texture and colour to handmade paper or cardmaking projects with dried flowers. Fresh flowers can be pressed and dried in a flower press or between absorbent paper weighted with books.

Polystyrene balls

With many uses, polystyrene balls are perfect for creating the round centres of paper flowers (see pp.156–61). They are available from craft stores and come in different sizes.

Floral wire

Made of flexible aluminium and commonly used to create the stems of paper flowers (see pp.156–61). Available from craft stores or floristry suppliers.

Mould and deckle

A key piece of equipment used in manual paper making (see pp.132–37). The mould is a framed screen, which 'catches' pulp to form a sheet of paper. You can learn how to make your own mould and deckle on p.134, or ready-made ones are available to buy from craft stores.

Quilling comb

A tool with long metallic teeth, used to create intricate, precise loops of quilled paper (see p.99). Create your own version of this tool with cocktail sticks or toothpicks.

Quilling tool

Used to coil paper strips to create basic shapes in quilling (see p.99). There are two common types: the slotted quilling tool and needle tool – both are used to secure the end of a quilling strip before it is rolled or curved into the required shape.

Circle sizer ruler

This is a circle gauge, used primarily to create consistently sized coils in quilling (see p.99). The ruler on the side can be used to measure each strip, to ensure they are the same length, before curling.

Craft punches and die-cutting machines

Available in many shapes and sizes, craft punches work in exactly the same way as a regular hole punch. They provide a fast and easy way to cut out many identical shapes from multiple sheets of paper in one go. Die-cutting machines are more of an investment, but can be used on a variety of materials besides paper, including fabric, foam sheets or even thin plastic.

Paper edgers

These are similar to pinking shears that are used on fabric. Using these special scissors with shaped blades will produce different effects, such as scallops or zigzags.

Other household items

Common household appliances such as an iron, blender and hand mixer are useful for many paper crafts, including papier mâché (see pp.150–53) and paper making (pp.132–37). Basic haberdashery equipment, including pins and needles, can also come in handy, as can some toolbox essentials, such as pliers, wire-cutters, sandpaper and paint brushes, though these are listed with the relevant projects where required. Disposable gloves are great to have on hand for messy jobs.

BASIC TECHNIQUES

Full instructions are given for each of the projects in this book, but there are a few basic techniques that are common to several of the projects that you will find it useful to be familiar with. Practise cutting, scoring and folding on pieces of scrap paper, so you can get used to your blade and the required pressure without wasting paper.

Using a scalpel or craft knife

Read the following techniques before embarking on the projects requiring a knife or blade. Refer also to the safety tips included on p.15.

1. Hold your craft knife or scalpel between your thumb and fingers, comfortably, as you would hold a pencil.

2. Practise shapes on a piece of scrap paper before embarking on the final project, so you can gauge the pressure required to create a clean cut.

3. Always cut out the trickiest or fiddliest elements first; if you are going to make mistakes it is best that you do this early on rather than on the last cut!

4. For curves and intricate shapes, you may find it easier to gently move the paper around the blade, rather than the other way around. This will be more comfortable, make cutting easier and allow you to be more accurate.

5. You can achieve a smoother motion by pulling the blade away from your body, from your elbow.

6. Change your blade as soon as it starts to feel dull (this could be as often as every 10–15 minutes). If your blade is dull then it will drag on the paper, and you are likely to make a mistake or injure yourself.

7. Do not press too hard or drag the knife or blade, as this can lead to uneven cuts and damaged blades. If your knife is dragging this is a sign you should change the blade.

8. Use the tip of your blade to gently stab and remove pieces of paper that have not fallen loose as you cut. Do not remove too much excess paper from the project, however, as it helps to strengthen the sheet and prevents your hand from accidentally snagging or tearing the design.

9. Metal scalpel handles and craft knives can make your hands sore if you are not used to holding them. For comfort, wrap a sticking plaster (Band-Aid) around the handle to cushion it against your fingers.

Scoring

Scoring means cutting the paper to about half its depth without cutting through. To practise scoring using scrap paper, run the blade, with varying amounts of pressure, over the paper, creating random lines. Fold those lines to see which ones hold well and which are sheared through or fall apart. This will give you a good idea of how much pressure to apply when scoring; the 'right' amount of pressure depends on the individual and the paper used, so take your time to work this out. Once you have a feel for how much pressure is needed, place a metal ruler next to the relevant line and very lightly draw the *back* of the blade down the ruler's edge (you can also use the edge of a bone folder or an empty ballpoint pen). Gently fold along the score line and press down firmly. Reinforce the fold by sliding a bone folder over the top.

Transferring images and templates

Many of the projects in this book have templates that may need to be transferred to paper. Certain templates may also need to be enlarged. There are several ways to do this.

Scanning and printing
The simplest way to transfer a template to paper is to scan the relevant template using a flat-bed scanner or photocopier scanner, then print the resulting scan to the reverse of your paper stock. Scanning and printing gives you the versatility to increase the scale when required and to adapt projects using desktop editing software.

Photocopying
Templates can be directly photocopied (and/or enlarged if necessary) onto printer paper or to the reverse of your chosen paper stock. A copy shop will be able to do this for you, given accurate instructions, if you do not have access to a photocopier.

Tracing
If you do not have access to a printer or photocopier, or a copy shop, tracing paper can be used to transfer images and templates (though not, easily, to enlarge them). Place your tracing paper over the top of the template and use a mechanical or sharp pencil to trace over the image with as much or little detail as needed. Turn over the paper and replicate the pencil lines exactly on the reverse. Now transfer the template to your paper by placing the tracing, right side up, over the paper, and rubbing a pencil over the traced lines; the design lines will now transfer to the paper underneath. Alternatively, you can use masking tape to secure your traced image over the top of your desired paper stock and cut through both layers at once.

Folding

To create crisp folds, draw your bone folder or the back of your scalpel along a metal ruler. Reinforce the fold by sliding a bone folder over the top. You may have seen references to different types of fold.

Mountain fold (left) Sometimes referred to as a peak fold, the fold is at the top, and the upper side of the paper is on the outside of the fold.

Valley fold (right) The fold is at the bottom and the upper side of the paper is enclosed in the fold.

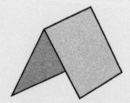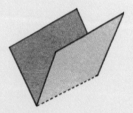

Accordion or concertina fold Parallel folds are created, alternating between mountain and valley. The piece will open out like an accordion.

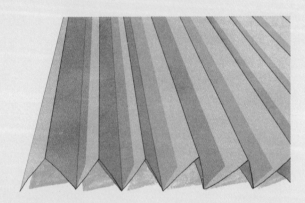

Gate fold Two parallel folds are made to create six panels – three panels on each side of the paper.

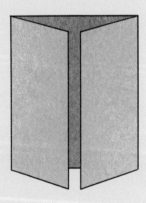

FOLDING

Take any kind of paper – from the printer, newspaper, even banknotes – and fold it. With just a few moves, this commonplace material transforms – its malleability enabling the creation of paper hats, boats, fans ... and countless more objects. Lightweight it may be, but paper can fold into surprisingly sturdy forms without breaking. And then, like magic, it can be unfolded again, with only its creases suggesting its previous incarnation.

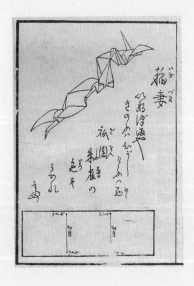

Facing page, top: Jun Mitani, traditional and 3D origami, 2017

Facing page, bottom: Jun Mitani, *Turbine*, 2012

Above: Annatomix and Sylvain Le Guen, *Fanometry*, 2017. Acrylic and ink on paper, Sipo wood

Left: A page from *Senbazuru Orikata* ('How to Fold One Thousand Cranes'), 1787

Although most closely associated with Japan, the art of paper folding probably originated in China, where funerary rites involve the use of paper replicas of money and household goods. Folded paper wasn't even generally known as 'origami' (from *oru*, to fold, and *kami*, paper) in Japan until the late nineteenth century.

Its first application in Japan was probably ceremonial – the folded white paper streamers, *o-shinde*, decorating Shinto temple entrances. Ise Sadatake's 1764 *Tsutsumi-no Ki* ('Notes on Wrapping and Tying', published as part of the wider manual of packaging, *Hoketsu zusetsu*, in 1840; p.32) outlines the ceremonial forms of folded wrappers, or *tsutsumi*, used in gift giving, from the wedding custom of attaching paper butterflies to a bride's and groom's sake glasses, to that of *noshi*, folded paper wrappers containing a strip of dried seafood and presented as a good-luck token.

Folded paper also had practical applications, and was made into containers for holding herbs and medicine, and even umbrellas. But it was the folded paper fan that became a major industry, exported to China and Europe from the fifteenth century, and reaching millions by the nineteenth. Not only for cooling their owners, the fans also came to be used as vehicles for written texts – conveying everything from court orders to educational texts – as well as works of art. As their popularity has subsequently dwindled, paper fan-making has become, today, an endangered craft. The 'Street Fans' project, launched in 2017 by London's Fan Museum, hopes to introduce the work of street artists into the fan-making tradition and popularize the form.

The emergence of paper folding as a recreational activity in Japan is evidenced by a 1734 ranma decorative wood panel – a classic feature of Japanese domestic architecture – now held at the Museum of Fine Arts, Boston, which includes the familiar forms of origami boats and cranes. *Senbazuru Orikata* ('How to Fold One Thousand Cranes'; p.21) is thought to be the oldest surviving text documenting recreational paper folding and was published in 1787, containing instructions for creating, in fact, forty-nine different cranes of varying

Facing page: Isoda Koryūsai,
Children folding a paper crane,
1772-73

Above: Won Park, Koi fish made
from a single one-dollar note,
2008

complexity. In the twentieth century, the origami crane became a global peace symbol, thanks to Sadako Sasaki's determination to fold a thousand cranes before her death, aged twelve, from leukemia – the result of exposure to radiation from the Hiroshima bombing. More recently, Romanian artist Cristian Marianciuc has folded a crane daily since 1 January 2015, using the process for reflection. 'Each time I look at one of my cranes, I can remember at least one thing about the day in which it was made,' he says.

Touring Japanese magicians brought origami-based tricks, subsequently recounted in Western publications, to Europe and North America in the second half of the nineteenth century. Even the famous American-Hungarian escapologist Harry Houdini penned a book on 'paper magic'. But, while European traditions including Spain's *Pajarita* (little bird) and elaborate napkin-folding techniques had been established for several centuries, it was German educationalist Friedrich Fröbel who was, eventually, the most influential. As the originator of the kindergarten system, his teachings – which included emphasizing the importance of paper folding for both maths and creativity – provided the theory underlying the

Japanese primary school curriculum from the 1890s. This not only ensured the art's continued practice, but also introduced new shapes such as 'Fröbel's star'. Although it now often carries his name, this geometric design – made from folding together four paper strips – actually probably pre-dates Fröbel. It's associated with Christmas in Germany and Nordic regions, and is popular in Japan because of its apparent resemblance to a chrysanthemum, a flower that is traditionally much loved.

The folding of banknotes, now known as 'moneygami', was first popularized by American troops in the Second World War, the uniform size of US notes being particularly suited to the pastime. The work is as intricate as the results among origami experts – each piece made by artist Won Park can take up to four hours. With computer software devised by the likes of Jun Mitani creating ever more advanced origami shapes, the range of its possible applications is also increasing. In July 2017 NASA put out an appeal for origami designs that could be adapted as protective folding shields for spacecraft, suggesting that this centuries-old craft has continuing relevance for the future.

PAPER FAN

'The Opera Fan', 1800

In the eighteenth century, the King's Theatre was London's primary opera house. Situated in the West End, where Her Majesty's Theatre stands today, it attracted wealthy patrons, who would rent theatre boxes to guarantee seats for themselves and their guests. A night at the opera was a social occasion and an opportunity to see and be seen, so it was important to know who might be attending the performances. The King's produced annual seating plans giving the names of the box holders; some of the plans were printed in a curved or semi-circular shape and were designed to be transformed into paper fans, giving the fashionable opera-goer a practical accessory while providing her with essential information for her evening out.

Wood and printed and glazed paper, 25 x 46.5 cm (10 x 18 in.)
V&A: S.1647–2014
Acquired with the support of the Friends of the V&A

PAPER FAN BUNTING

An easy, fun project to get stuck into; you probably used a technique like this as a child to make something you could fan yourself with on a hot day – this is almost the same method, but used to transform paper into a beautiful and unique decoration. You can buy new materials – a pack of printed craft paper squares is ideal – but this project is also perfect for using up old wrapping paper or similar. The instructions are to make 1 m (3¼ ft) of bunting, but you can expand as you wish!

Project by Clare Pentlow

You will need

4 sheets craft paper, each 30.5 x 30.5 cm (12 x 12 in.). **Note:** *Almost any weight of paper will work, though avoid thick card, as it will be difficult to fold neatly.*
Scissors
Hand-sewing cotton
Glue stick, or PVA glue and applicator
Paperclips
Hole punch
1.45 m (4¾ ft) ribbon/string
Ruler
Pencil

How to make

Tie the centre of the concertina with a length of cotton, before gluing the sides together to create a circular fan shape.

1 Start with one square sheet of craft paper, fold and then cut in half along the fold.

2 Take one half of the sheet and fold in half, lengthwise, repeatedly, until the width of the resulting strip is roughly 1 cm (½ in.)

3 Unfold and then fold again, this time creating a concertina (right), with the most decorative side of the paper facing up and the two end folds forming 'mountains' rather than 'valleys' (see p.19).

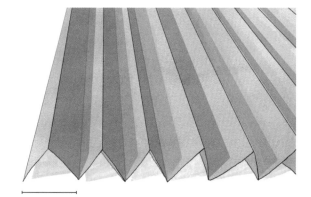

Mountain

4 Gather the concertina into a strip again and then fold in half in the centre, making the fold in both directions. Use a strand of cotton to tie the strip at this fold, creating a bow-tie-like shape.

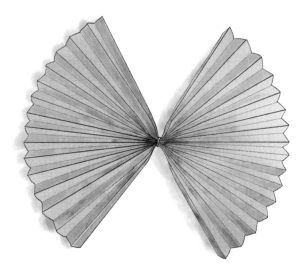

5 Glue together the edges that meet when the two sides of the fan are opened out, to form a completely circular decoration. Hold the glued edges in place with paperclips while the glue dries, if necessary.

6 Repeat until you have as many circles as necessary to create your bunting (eight should be enough to make 1 m/3¼ ft of bunting). Punch a hole in the glued section of each, on both sides, and thread the fans onto your piece of ribbon or string to complete the bunting.

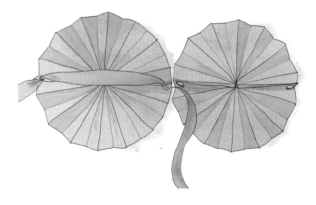

Now try...

Creating different kinds of bunting by using different gluing and folding techniques. For example, if, at step 4, you simply glue one set of the fan edges together, you can make semi-circular decorations (below, left). You then need only punch holes on each side of each fan and join these two 'corners' with ribbon or string.

Decorations made using quarter-sheets of paper and glued together along their outside edges in an alternating right-side-up/upside-down pattern will form a long bunting that need only be secured by ties at each end (below, right).

ORIGAMI

Ise Sadatake, *Tsutsumi-no Ki* ('Notes on Wrapping and Tying'), 1764 (1840)

The origins of origami are much disputed, partly as a result of the inherently short lifespan of the paper results themselves. While it is thought that paper itself was brought to Japan from Buddhist China and Korea in the sixth century AD, it is not known whether the art of folding paper developed independently in Japan or was in fact based on an earlier, existing tradition from one of these countries. We do know that the earliest written reference to origami dates from 1680 – a short poem by Ikara Saikaku refers to the *Ocho Mecho* (Male and Female Butterflies) origami model, used to decorate sake bottles at Shinto weddings – during a 'boom period' for paper in Japan, when the material was produced plentifully by local industry.

Ise Sadatake's 1764 guide to ceremonial origami, *Tsutsumi-no Ki*, was incorporated into the later (1840) publication *Hoketsu zusetsu*, pictured here. This Japanese manual of packaging techniques includes reference to *Ocho Mecho*, as well as to other long-established samurai traditions, such as the giving of *noshi* – folded paper wrappers, historically filled with dried seafood – as a good-luck token.

Woodblock-printed book, 26.8 x 18.2 cm (10½ x 7 in.)
Museum of Fine Arts, Boston: 2011.1466

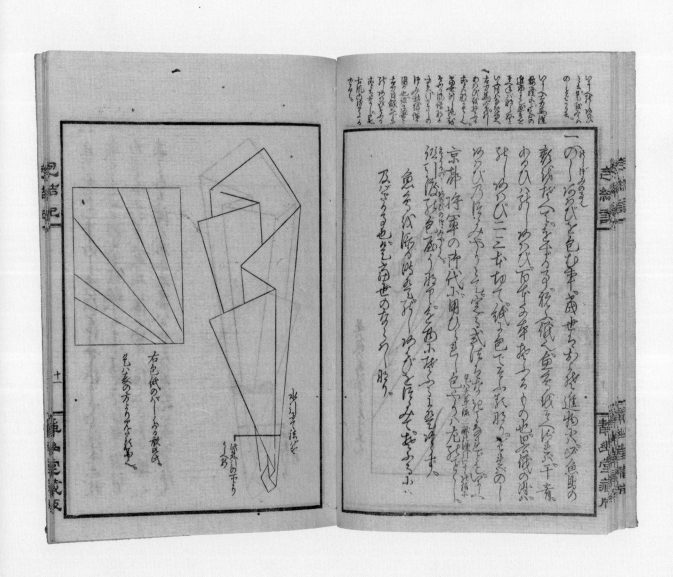

'MONEYGAMI' OUTFITS

This simple origami project will introduce you to some basic folding techniques, allowing you to create the colourful little outfits shown opposite. The use of paper money to create folded-paper artworks – 'moneygami' – has its origins in the early twentieth century (see p.25), and is a fun twist on the ancient techniques of origami proper, but of course you can use any lightweight, crisp paper to create these decorative outfits.

Project by Samuel Tsang

You will need

Selection of paper banknotes (1 per item of 'clothing'), ideally in a variety of colours. **Note:** *The size of your notes doesn't really matter, but bear in mind that it will affect the size of the resulting 'clothes'. So, for example, use notes of a consistent size if you want to make several 'shirts' of a consistent size.*

Optional

Bone folder or ruler

How to make

To make a 'shirt'

1 Take one note and lay it horizontally, 'face up' on your work surface. Fold it in half lengthwise, creating a valley fold (see p.19). Unfold again and lay the note flat. **Tip:** *A bone folder or the edge of a ruler will help to make your folds more crisp, but is not essential!*

2 Now 'mountain fold' the note (fold it backwards, or away from you), creating a vertical fold a third of the way along its length. Leave this fold in place.

3 Fold the top and bottom long edges of the note inwards towards the central crease made in step 1, creating two valley folds.

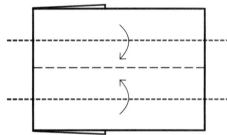

4 As shown in the illustration below, fold the inner left-hand corners of the note – those on either side of the central fold – outwards, creating your 'sleeves'.

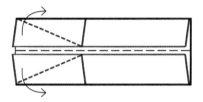

5 To form the collar, make a small mountain fold at the opposite end of the note, turning a small segment of the note towards the back.

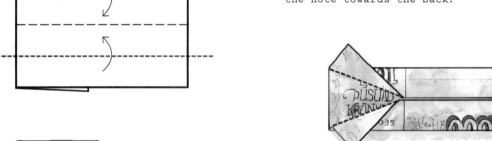

Using notes from different currencies will give you different effects, with varying colours and motifs.

6 Fold in the two right-hand outer corners of the note, so that the tips of these folds meet at the centre line, making two diagonal valley folds towards the centre. The outer edges of your folds should run about a third of the way along the long edges of the note.

7 Create a soft valley fold roughly at the point where the lip made in step 2 appears, taking the right-hand side of your note over to the left. Tuck the flat edge under the tips of your collar to finish your shirt. **Note:** *You may have to slightly adjust the first fold made in this step in order to achieve this, depending on the original size and proportions of your note, which is why you should make it a 'soft' fold in the first instance.*

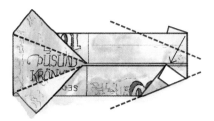

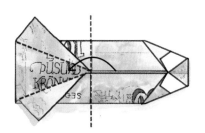

Fold up a pair of trousers or a skirt to complete the outfit.

To make a 'skirt'

1 Take one note and lay it vertically, 'face up' on your work surface. Make a valley fold approx. 1 cm (½ in.) from the bottom edge of the note.

2 Turn your note over and repeat the valley fold. Continue to repeat the valley fold on alternate sides of the note until you have folded the entire note and created a concertina.

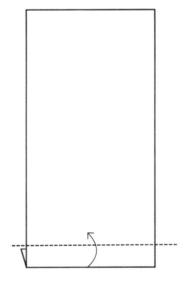

3 Pinch together one end of the concertina and spread the other. Making a fold at the pinched end will secure your finished skirt shape. You can now insert the skirt into the slot formed at the bottom of the shirt, to create a full figure (see photograph, p.35).

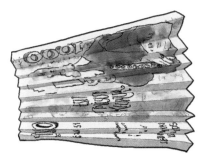

Now try...

Using paper in different sizes, shapes and colours. You will achieve a different end result and different clothing proportions depending on your original choice of paper; experiment to achieve a variety of results. You could even make a large, frameable version, using posters or similar as your raw material!

To make 'trousers'

1 Take one note and lay it horizontally, 'face up' on your work surface. Fold it in half lengthwise, creating a valley fold.

2 Valley fold the note in half again lengthwise, bringing the bottom folded edge up to meet the top edges of the note.

3 To finish your trousers, create a diagonal valley fold halfway along the length of your folded strip, as per the illustration below. You can now insert the trousers into the slot formed at the bottom of the shirt, to create a full figure (see photograph, p.35).

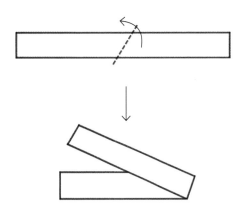

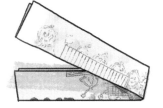

PLEATED ORIGAMI VASE COVER

This sculptural origami construction wraps around a plant pot or vase, to striking effect. The key to this project is patience! A template is provided on p.45, with all fold lines marked. Take your time and be sure to follow the diagram so that you know which are mountain and which are valley folds (see p.19). You can enlarge (or reduce) the template to any size you wish to create a larger (or smaller) vase.

Project by Ankon Mitra

You will need

1 x A2 sheet non-fibrous medium-to-heavyweight paper (not handmade or recycled), minimum 200 gsm
Craft scissors
Cutting mat
Safety cutter with stainless-steel snap blades (or scalpel/craft knife)
Bone folder
Metal ruler
15-20 bulldog/binder clips, 15 mm (½ in.)
5-6 rubber bands
PVA glue and applicator
Paperclips

How to make

1 Photocopy or otherwise enlarge the template on p.45 to full size and transfer to your A2 sheet (see p.19 for further instructions). **Tip:** *You might want to get this done at a copy shop to save time. You can, in fact, enlarge the pattern to any size desired.*

2 Cut away the margins of the design — a neat rectangle containing the folding pattern should remain.

3 Place the sheet horizontally on the cutting mat and lightly score all pattern lines using your metal ruler and safety cutter (see p.18 for scoring tips).

4 The two types of line on the pattern are 'mountains' (solid lines) and 'valleys' (dashed lines). Fold along the lines, following the illustration below, changing direction according to the kind of line you are working with (see below and p.19). You will notice that the vertical lines on the pattern are alternately marked as mountains and valleys. There is a trick here: as you would fold a simple pleated fan, each vertical line on the sheet, from top to bottom, can first be folded completely as a mountain, and then also as a valley. This makes the fold flexible, like a hinge, and means they can later be folded in the correct directions more simply. For the zigzag or horizontal lines, there is no trick. Fold them line by line as per the notation on the pattern.

Mountain

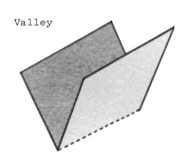

Valley

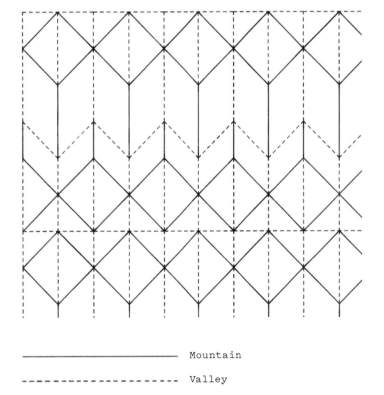

————————————— Mountain

- - - - - - - - - - - - - - - Valley

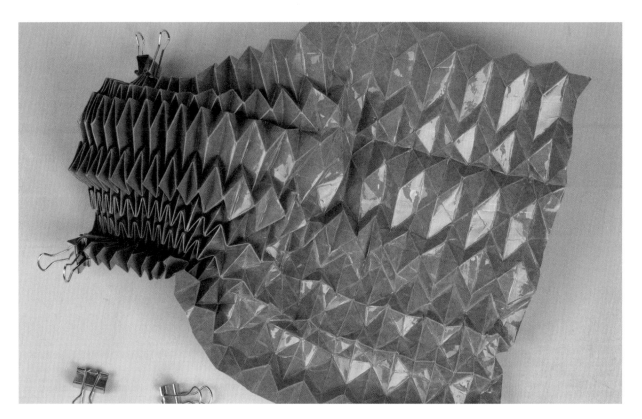

Carefully complete all of the mountain and valley folds, following the diagram.
Collapse the sheet and hold sections in place with bulldog clips.

5   Turn the sheet over. It is still
flat but you will be able to 'read'
the mountains and valleys.

6   Begin collapsing the sheet, slowly,
from one end, gathering the folds into
pleats as you go along. This is the most
challenging and frustrating part of the
exercise – don't give up! Use the bone
folder to press down 3-4 pleated folds
in one go, securing areas of folds using
bulldog/binder clips; this frees your
fingers to start folding and collapsing
the next section. (Release the clips
temporarily if they are constraining your
work on the next section, then reattach
when the folds look resolved.)

7   When you have finished pleating the
entire sheet, remove all the clips and
wind rubber bands tightly around the
various segments – this is a state of
complete collapse into folds called 'flat
foldability'. The rubber bands help to
make the folds permanent.

Rubber bands will hold the paper in a state of flat foldability
- this will ensure that folds are permanent.

8   After 10-15 minutes, remove the rubber bands and lightly stretch the sheet out like an accordion.

9   You are now ready to make up your vase, with the printed side of the sheet on the inside. Roll the pleated sheet into cylindrical form and overlap the end areas (you will notice they fit snugly, one end into the other). Apply PVA glue to one side of the join and hold the two parts together with your fingers or paperclips until the glue is dry.

Now try...

Different shapes. If, instead of closing the sheet like a cylinder, you gather the pleats on one side of the sheet and glue and staple them together, you will make an elaborate Japanese fan. Rolling the sheet so that opposite diagonal corners are brought together, and gluing, creates conch-shell-like forms that look beautiful hung as a mobile. An elaborate, sculptural piece, resembling an Elizabethan ruff, can be created by pulling together two corners on the same side of the sheet, creating a loop and a flaring outline on the opposite side.

Template

Template shown at 33% (enlarge to 300%)

CUTTING

To make their mark, the papercutter needs little more than a blade and paper. Employing these simple tools, this art has been practised across many centuries and cultures. While paper may tear easily, it can be cut with ease and precision. We're all familiar with using a pencil to navigate a piece of paper – how about substituting it for a blade to explore and reimagine what that paper could become?

Facing page, top: Lisa Lloyd, *Blue Tit*, 2017

Facing page, bottom: Augustin Edouart, 'The Coghlan Family' silhouette, early 19th century, France
41 x 56.5 cm (16¼ x 22¼ in.)
V&A: P.4-1947. Given by Mrs M.E.M. Coghlan

Above: Mexican *papel picado* decoration, San Miguel de Allende, Mexico, 2009

Left: Paper peepshow, 'The River Thames and Tunnel', c. 1843
Front panel: 18 x 23.5 cm (7 x 9¼ in.), expands to approx. 79 cm (31 in.)
National Art Library, V&A: Gestetner 238

Art created by a blade cutting paper: over centuries, around the world, this simple technique has inspired countless variations. In China alone, a rich diversity of designs has developed over the hundreds of years that papercutting has been practised, from the world's oldest surviving example – a simple symmetrical design, dating to the fifth century, found in the Xinjiang region – to today, when imagery can encompass the likes of mythological characters, exquisite butterflies, pomegranates and peonies, and even everyday scenes from rural life, cut both by skilled amateurs and in professional workshops.

The craft's accessibility has inspired inventiveness in both tools and subject matter. The penknife – initially so-called because it sharpened quill pens used for writing – found new use in papercutting; in Germany, the technique is known as *Scherenschnitte*, referring to the 'scissor cuts' traditionally used for the art; shears – first used to cut patterns in bark and leather – create Poland's distinctive *wycinanki*; while chisels and punches, cutting through several sheets simultaneously, make Mexico's colourful *papel picado* (punched paper).

Both *papel picado* and *wycinanki* – like the Chinese *chuāng huā*, or 'window flowers' – were created to be decorative, adorning windows, walls and, in the case of *papel picado*, streets and altars on festive occasions. In contemporary practice, the American street artist Swoon wheat-pastes her large-scale paper-cut scenes onto urban buildings, to interact – in her words – with 'the naturally occurring collage of the city'. Cut paper has been used to create objects of religious significance, such as intricate papercut Mizrahi – plaques indicating the direction of prayer – made by Ashkenazi Jews since the eighteenth century, as well as pieces for personal reflection, whether in the form of a

Facing page: Bovey Lee, *Bonsai – Wired Cities* (detail), 2016
Cut Chinese *xuan* (rice) paper on silk,
59 x 66 cm (23¼ x 26 in.)

Above: Multi-coloured traditional *wycinanki* papercut from the Łowicz region of Poland, artist unknown, 2007

Left: Paper-Cut-Project (Amy Flurry & Nikki Nye) for Red Valentino boutique, Milan, 2013

The Lord's Prayer

THE LORDS PRAYER
OUR FATHER WHICH ART IN HEA
VEN HALLOWED BE THY NAME THY
KINGDOM COME THY WILL BE DONE
IN EARTH AS IT IS IN HEAVEN GIVE US
THIS DAY OUR DAILY BREAD AND FOR -
GIVE US OUR TRESPASSES AS WE FOR-
GIVE THEM THAT TRESPASS AGAINST
US AND LEAD US NOT INTO TEMPTATION
BUT DELIVER US FROM EVIL FOR THINE
IS THE KINGDOM THE POWER AND
THE GLORY FOR EVER AND
EVER AMEN

painstakingly cut-out version of the Lord's Prayer, made in Britain, or the Dutch and Germanic tradition of cut-paper cards – especially homemade Valentines. It has a practical role elsewhere: while cut paper in Japan has developed into an elaborate art known as kirigami, the earliest examples were stencils for textile dyeing; today, the artist Rob Ryan sometimes translates his papercuts into stencils for screen-prints, making his work available to a wider audience.

Before photography, papercutting could also offer a means of record and display. In both Europe and North America, from the mid-eighteenth century onwards, cut-paper silhouettes – scenes in a single colour, often black – became hugely popular as a cheaper, and accessible, alternative to painted portraits, just as peepshows and tunnel books (see p.78) were embraced in the following century as a way of commemorating and promoting significant events, like coronations, and modern wonders, such as the Crystal Palace created for London's Great Exhibition of 1851. The making of these cut and decorated paper scenes, which expand out,

accordion-style, to create an illusion of depth, was undertaken both commercially and by amateurs, as an inexpensive pastime. In 1835, professional silhouette artist Augustin Edouart passed on his cutting advice, advising the avoidance of strong tea, coffee and spirits, 'to preserve a steady hand'.

Also, of course, papercutting can be used for explorations of the imagination. Danish author Hans Christian Andersen was known to improvise stories aloud as he cut scenes from paper. His fairy tales continue to inspire artists such as Vicki Zoe, who transforms paper-cut silhouettes into mobiles, with the stated aim of letting the 'imagination flow freely'.

Throughout history, papercutting has been largely anonymous. Contemporary Chinese-American artist Bovey Lee references its unnamed, frequently female, makers. Although little is known about these individuals, the pieces created can still inspire our wonder many centuries later, as we – in Lee's words – marvel at those with the skill and dedication to create 'such intricate and labour-intensive works by hand'.

Facing page, top: T. Hunter, 'The Lord's Prayer', 1786, Great Britain
Cut-paper work on a blue paper ground, 17 x 14 cm (6½ x 5½ in.)
V&A: E.115-1928. Given by Queen Mary

Facing page, bottom: Papercut of a cat, 1985, China
Cut paper, 10 x 14 cm (4 x 5½ in.)
V&A: FE.130-1992

Above: Swoon, *Family Feeding Pigeons*, 2000s, blockprint on paper pasted to a wall

PAPERCUTTING

Papercut, 1986

Chinese papercuts are made with either scissors or a small sharp knife. When a knife is used the paper is often held against a wax-covered board, giving the maker extra purchase for this fine work. Finished pieces are traditionally pasted onto paper windows as seasonal decorations, most often during Chinese New Year. Papercuts are designed to be backlit. When pasted upon a window with an interior light source, light shines through the cut-out areas, picking out the design as a silhouette. In this piece thin cuts on the lark's neck and wings illuminate its plumage, while wider cuts on the bird's breast describe the feathers on its chest. This papercut is made of white paper that has been dyed in a bold palette of pinks, blues, yellows and greens. The colour adds greater clarity to the design, separating the different elements of the lark, flowers, fish, foliage and seasonal red tassels. The image of the fish is a metaphor for abundance commonly seen in New Year decorations, as the Chinese word *yü* means both 'fish' and 'surplus'.

Papercut depicting symbols of abundance, Fengning, China, 9.5 x 15 cm (3¾ x 6 in.) V&A: FE.143-1992

TROPICAL BIRDS PAPERCUT

Learn the art of papercutting using this layered template with a tropical theme. The project has been designed in three separate layers to help you learn core skills and develop your papercutting technique – from beginner through to advanced – as you work through the steps. All three layers are brought together at the end to create a stunning finished piece that will fit in an A4-size frame.

Project by Samantha Quinn

You will need

4 sheets A4 coloured paper (4 separate colours), 110-160 gsm. See photograph for suggested colours
Cutting mat
Craft knife or scalpel, with blades
Metal ruler
PVA glue
Toothpick/cocktail stick
2-3 sheets A4 white copy paper (scrap will do)
Masking or washi tape

Optional, for in-fills (see p.58)

3 sheets A4 coloured or patterned mid-weight paper, 110-160 gsm. Colours to contrast with those used for the main papercut

How to make

1   Photocopy or otherwise transfer each layer of the cutting template on pp.59-60 to the reverse of your coloured paper sheets, enlarging to 100% (see p.19 for full instructions). Choose a different colour for each layer and set the fourth colour/sheet aside for the background of the papercut. **Note:** *Make sure every layer is transferred at the same size.*

Top layer (beginner)

2   Place the first sheet – printed with the 'top layer' template – in the centre of your cutting mat. Start cutting away the white, unprinted areas, beginning with the curves of the leaf shapes, which should be cut from the branch outwards towards the tip of each leaf. Use your craft knife or scalpel, holding it in the same position and rotating your paper as you work. This will help you keep the blade upright and ensure maximum precision.

3   The circles and curves in each corner of the template should be cut next. Move your scalpel in a smooth motion and, again, rotate the paper to create clean curves. Remove cut pieces as you go with the tip of your scalpel.

4   Next, use a metal ruler with your blade to cut the straight lines of the 'branches' and the inside edge of the template border.

5   The last element to cut is the outer edge of the border, again using your metal ruler (the same applies for every layer – the outer edge of the border should always be cut last).

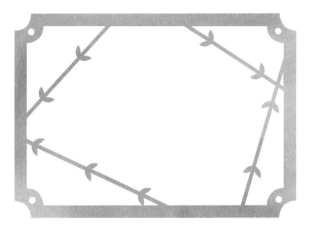

Middle layer (intermediate)

6   This template is designed to introduce you to finer lines and more intricate shapes. Start with the smallest, trickiest cut-outs – the internal shapes of the birds, working each body from the top down. By cutting the internal shapes first, you will preserve the stability of your papercut for as long as possible.

7   Next, cut the inner section of each leaf, followed by the outer curves of the leaves. Move on to the waves and curved edges of the border, pulling the scalpel towards you and rotating your wrist in a smooth and controlled motion.

8   Use a metal ruler to cut the straight lines of the branches.

Cut out the layers one by one, starting with the top (beginner) layer.

9 Finally, carefully cut the outer shape of each bird, steadying the papercut with your fingers as you remove the remaining negative paper shapes.

Bottom layer (advanced)

10 Cut the smaller internal shapes between leaves and flowers first. Start in one corner and carefully cut out and remove the internal shapes, moving in one direction across the template (towards your working hand is best, so that it doesn't move over and damage areas that have been cut).

11 Once the internal shapes have been cut, cut out the larger area in the centre of the template. Steady the paper using your non-cutting hand as you go.

12 Lastly, use a metal ruler to cut the straight edges of the outer border.

Adding in-fills (optional)

13 In-fills are a nice way of embellishing
your papercut by adding colours or pattern
to small sections. The in-fill templates
on p.61 will allow you to add colours to
the middle layer. Transfer the templates
to your coloured paper as before and cut
out the shapes. Place the middle layer
of your papercut (with the birds) onto
your cutting mat, face down. Position your
cut-out in-fill shapes over the bodies and
wings of the birds, using the diagram on
p.60 as a guide. Using a toothpick, apply
small dots of PVA glue to the back of the
papercut, and glue the in-fills in place.
Allow to dry.

Layering your finished papercut

14 Start by positioning your cut layers
on top of each other to get an idea of how
the composition will look.

15 Take the fourth sheet of coloured paper,
which you previously set aside, and use
this as your background. Apply tiny dots
of glue to the reverse (printed side) of the
bottom (advanced) layer using a toothpick
or cocktail stick. Turn over and position
in the centre of your backing sheet. Place
an A4 sheet of blank copy paper over the
top and press down to secure the layer in
position (you will need to use a separate
sheet for each layer, to avoid getting glue
on visible parts of the papercut).

16 Repeat with the middle (intermediate)
and top (beginner) layers, carefully
positioning each one centrally over
the last. Allow to dry.

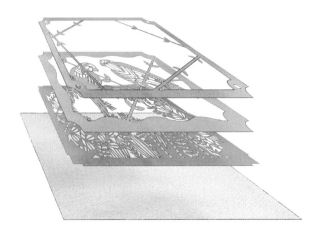

Now try...

A 3D version. It's possible to add depth to your
layered papercut by assembling the layers using
double-sided foam 'spacers' (sticky foam pads,
which are available at most craft suppliers).
Working from the bottom layer upwards, attach
the foam pads to the papercut borders on each
layer (use around four on each edge, including
the corners) and to larger areas that will overlap
with the layer below. The top layer does not need
foam pads, just a few dots of glue. The final
result is very striking.

Add interest to your finished papercut by adding
in-fills and/or 3D spacers.

Cutting templates

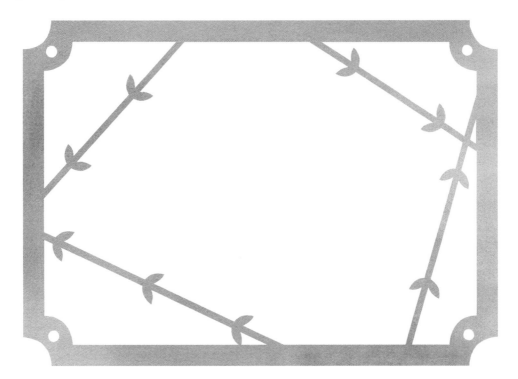

Top layer (beginner)

Middle layer (intermediate)

Templates shown at 50% (enlarge to 200%)

Bottom layer (advanced)

Template shown at 50% (enlarge to 200%)

In-fill diagram

In-fill templates

Templates shown at 100%

WYCINANKI

Wycinanki papercut, 2008

Pronounced 'vee-chee-nan-kee', the origins of this Polish
technique are obscure, but most sources seem to agree that
they were relatively humble, with the earliest designs executed
in rural areas using sheep shears, the only cutting implement
available. Decorative paper banners and medallions made in
this way were traditionally used as domestic ornaments (very
effective when set against whitewashed walls), given as gifts
and made to celebrate religious holidays, with rural scenes
and geometric designs predominating. Popular from the mid-
nineteenth century onwards (and practised especially widely
during the communist era), *wycinanki* is most closely associated
with the Kurpie and Łowicz regions; the multi-coloured, layered
designs of the latter inspired the project overleaf. The example
shown here – a *gwiazdy*, or medallion, from Łowicz – features a
cockerel motif, traditionally associated with the Easter period.

Helena Miazek
Cut paper, Łowicz, Poland, 56 x 56 cm (22 x 22 in.)
The Horniman Museum and Gardens, London

WYCINANKI-INSPIRED CARDS

The shapes and colours of traditional Polish papercutting inspired these bright, bold cards, which, with their semi-abstract designs, can be used for almost any occasion. This project is a good opportunity to practise your scissor or scalpel skills, as it does require some patience and dexterity, but the card construction itself is very simple and the results are impressive. The motifs can be arranged in a variety of compositions.

Project by Clare Pentlow

You will need

Lightweight (90 gsm) copy paper in a range of colours

Scissors

Glue stick

Pencil

Ruler

Eraser

Square-format blank cards, 15 x 15 cm (6 x 6 in.). You can buy these or make your own from A3 white card cut to size and folded in half.

Optional

Scalpel with blades

Cutting mat

How to make

Transfer the templates onto coloured paper, fold as indicated, and then carefully cut out the shapes.

1 Assemble the coloured papers needed to create your chosen card design. You can either re-create the designs shown here, or improvise your own.

Note: *You may need up to a single separate sheet of paper for each pair of design elements (see templates on p.69). For example, if making card A (p.65, top), for which you require 4 of the large 'fan' shape (C) in red, you may need 2 sheets of red paper, depending on the size of sheet chosen. In total, up to 24 sheets in 9 colours are required for card A and 17 sheets in 11 colours for card B (p.65, bottom).*

2 Photocopy, or otherwise transfer, the relevant templates A-E from p.69 onto your coloured paper sheets, at 100% size. As noted above, remember that two of each shape will be created by each template. Templates A-C include different size options. **Note:** *Not all the shapes on the templates are required for each card design, so take care when selecting which shape to cut. You may prefer to cut out a selection of shapes and experiment.*

3 To create each pair of shapes, first roughly cut around the outer edge of the template. Fold the paper piece in half lengthwise along the dashed line of the template, and then in half again along the dotted line, keeping the black cutting outline visible and facing towards you (see photograph opposite).

4 Cut out the relevant shape for your design, using scissors or a scalpel and cutting mat, then unfold and flatten the resulting cut-outs. **Tip:** *Start with the largest shape of each design element, working down to the smaller shapes.*

5 Once all shapes have been cut for a particular design element, glue them together, lining up the fold lines on each and remembering to keep the cutting outlines to the wrong side.

6 You can make more use of each paper sheet, and create a positive and negative effect, by cutting into the paper templates as shown below. This will result in spaces in each design element through which the blank card can be seen.

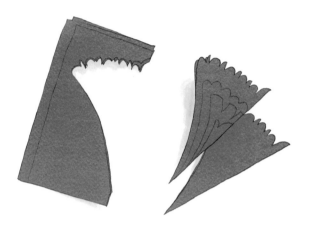

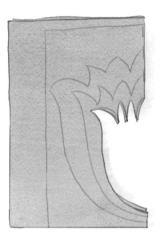

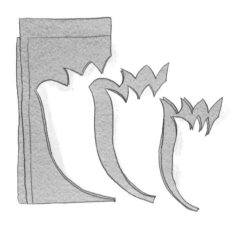

Experiment with layout. Create a 3D effect with the layered
shapes (left) or try using negative space (right).

7   Using a ruler and pencil, lightly
mark the centre of a blank card. You
can sub-divide the card further to aid
in positioning the design elements, but
remember that you will have to rub out
all of these markings before you glue
the elements in place.

8   Position and glue down all design
elements. Erase any visible pencil marks.

Now try...

**Making three-dimensional versions of these
designs.** Cut six or more of the same shape in
various colours, keeping them folded, and glue
the shapes together in 'book' form along the
central folds. Once glued to your card, they will
appear like an open book, with 'pages' standing
proud of the card (see photograph above).

Design templates

A

B

C

D

E

Templates shown at 100%

SILHOUETTES

Cut-paper silhouettes, *c.* 1820–28

From the eighteenth century onwards, the art of papercutting
was considered an appropriate pastime for women in the home.
Laura Muir Mackenzie, the daughter of a prominent family
from Perthshire, Scotland, was a talented amateur cutter of
paper silhouettes. She produced much of her work while in her
teens, principally cutting group silhouettes of domestic scenes,
such as this family portrait. Using her friends and relations
as models, Mackenzie's silhouettes depict subjects including
mothers with babies, children playing games, women doing
needlework and rural scenes. The scene opposite showing an
unknown family group is cut from a single piece of white paper:
black paper was not available before 1826 and until then, artists
had to blacken their own paper, most often using 'lamp black',
a pigment made by collecting soot from oil lamps.

Laura Muir Mackenzie.
Opposite: Unknown Family Group
Cut paper, Scotland, 15 x 20 cm (6 x 8 in.)
V&A: P.58-1930.
Below: 'A Stag Hunt'
Cut paper, 11 x 17 cm (4¼ x 6¾ in.)
V&A: P.59-1930. Given by the Hon. Frances M. Talbot

FAMILY AND FRIENDS SILHOUETTE

Although a silhouette contains no surface detail, it is still possible to convey both the likeness and personality of a portrait subject or group through this simple papercutting method. This project aims to inspire you to create your own silhouette portrait of family and friends. First experiment with the templates provided here (there are two levels of complexity to try), then follow the instructions given on p.76 to create your own, original work. Your finished piece will fit in an A4-size frame.

Project by Roma McLaughlin

You will need

Cutting mat
1 sheet lightweight A4 black paper, 80-120 gsm
1 sheet lightweight A4 white copy paper, max. 80 gsm, for templates
1 sheet mid-weight A4 white craft paper, min. 120 gsm, for background
Sticky tape
Craft knife or scalpel, with blades
Metal ruler
Pencil
Eraser
PVA glue
Toothpick or cocktail stick
A4 picture frame

For your own family portrait

A family photograph (see step 9 for tips on choosing a photo)
Photocopier or scanner
Paper and frame, as above, to desired size

How to make

1 Photocopy or trace the cutting template from p.77 onto an A4 sheet of max. 80 gsm copy paper (see p.19 for full instructions). There are two cutting options to choose from – one simple, and the other more complex and detailed – as indicated by the black and grey areas of the template, respectively. You can choose whether to cut out the full template or the black shapes only.

2 Place the template over your sheet of black paper and attach both to your cutting mat with sticky tape placed over the corners (take care not to place tape over the image area).

3 You can see that the dark, positive, shapes in the templates are all connected, no element of the silhouette is 'floating'. Start cutting away the white, negative shapes using your scalpel – begin with the smallest areas, to help prevent your paper from tearing. You will be cutting through both the template sheet and black paper simultaneously. **Tip:** *Before cutting into your template, you may wish to practise cutting some basic shapes. Continue to work until all of the white paper is cut away, using a metal ruler with your scalpel for any straight lines.*

4 Carefully remove your template and finished papercut from the cutting mat and separate the two.

5 Fixing mistakes is easier than you might think. If you've cut too much or too far, you can mend the area from the back. Simply dot glue onto the papercut surface using a toothpick or cocktail stick, then 'patch' the area using a tiny strip or scrap of the black paper.

Papercutting tips

Anchor the cutting mat with one hand, and work with the blade in your other, holding it vertically, like a pencil, for greater precision. It will help you to keep the blade straight if you move the whole mat around while cutting different shapes. You can also achieve a smoother motion by pulling the blade away from you, with your elbow. Remove cut shapes using the tip of your blade. See pp.18 and 56–58 for further papercutting and scalpel-handling tips.

Secure your work before you begin cutting. Fix the template and the black paper in place on the cutting mat with a piece of tape at each corner.

6　Place the finished silhouette centrally onto your A4 white background paper sheet and mark its position lightly with pencil dots (these can be erased later).

7　Turn the silhouette over and, again using PVA glue and a toothpick or cocktail stick, dot glue onto the reverse (you don't need to cover the surface with glue — this should be enough). Position the silhouette, right side up, in line with your previous pencil marks, and smooth down onto the backing sheet. Leave to dry completely.

8　You can now frame your finished artwork. **Note:** *If you use a box frame, your papercut silhouette may 'float' and curl away from the background, creating shadows. You will need to use a flat frame, sandwiching the silhouette between glass and backing, if you want to avoid this result. It is possible, on the other hand, to accentuate the 'shadow' effect by securing your cut, black-paper silhouette between two sheets of thin glass rather than gluing it to the backing sheet in step 7, and then framing this construction.*

Whether you choose to cut the full, complex template (above left),
or the simpler partial template (above right), a picture frame will
protect your finished piece.

Going further: a family portrait

9 You can personalize this project by
using your own family or group photograph
to create a unique template. Choose a
photograph in which individuals or a
group are silhouetted, with their outlines
clearly visible (photographs taken against
a wall or plain background work best) –
ideally, individual silhouettes would just
join or overlap within a group composition,
so that they remain recognizable. Photocopy
and enlarge the photograph if necessary,
and then trace the relevant outlines to
a plain white sheet of 80 gsm (lightweight)
paper, which will act as your template.

10 Follow steps 2-7 using this new
template to create your own, personalized
silhouette.

Now try...

Different subjects and colour palettes.
You don't have to use black for your silhouettes –
experiment with different paper colours for
both the cut-out and the background to change
the mood of your finished piece. Likewise, you
don't have to stick to people: buildings, trees,
animals and plants – in fact, anything with a
detailed, recognizable outline – can make for
a good silhouette.

Cutting template

Template shown at 100%

PEEPSHOWS

Teleorama no. 1, c. 1825

Paper peepshows resemble pocket-sized stage sets, complete with backdrop and paper cut-out scenes linked by folding bellows, which expand to create an illusion of depth. They were a cheap form of optical toy that appeared in the 1820s, at first in Germany and Austria. Most commonly sold as souvenirs, they might celebrate particular events, famous places or feats of engineering. This early example, expanding to c. 66 cm (26 in.) in depth, was published around 1825. As one peeps through the branches of a tree, a bucolic vista unfolds, dotted with characters such as shepherds and their flocks. The eye is led towards the back panel, on which a large country house is depicted, with ladies rowing across a nearby stream. It is part of the newly acquired Gestetner collection at the National Art Library, part of the V&A.

Published by Heinrich Friedrich Müller, Vienna, Austria
Hand-coloured etchings on paper, cardboard and paper bellows, front panel: 11.8 x 14.5 cm (4¾ x 5¾ in.), length: approx. 66 cm (26 in.; extended)
National Art Library, V&A: Gestetner 1

LANDSCAPE PEEPSHOW

Paper peepshows, also known as tunnel books or theatre books, are a great, relatively simple way to capture a memory or depict a scene. Layered paper panels, attached to two concertina-folded side structures, create a 3D effect. This project makes use of found images to take the viewer on a walk through the woods. You can choose to use the templates provided, or your own subject and images. The construction is simpler than it looks – in fact, the trickiest bit of this project is probably the papercutting involved in creating the individual scenes.

Project by Clare Bryan

You will need

1 x A4 sheet thin card or heavyweight white paper, 200 gsm
Craft knife or scalpel, with blades
Small pair craft scissors
Cutting mat
6 x A4 sheets mid-weight white paper, 160 gsm
Metal ruler
Sharp pencil
Bone folder
PVA glue and brush
1 piece paper or card, 160-200 gsm, 60 x 15 cm (23½ x 6 in.), for cover

Optional

Colour printer/photocopier
Image selection, to decorate scenic panels (see step 3 for notes on how to select images)
Circle cutter, suitable for paper
Paints, colouring pens or crayons

How to make

1 First, cut out panels A and B to size (see illustration below) from the heavier (200 gsm) A4 paper or card. The panels are the same size, but panel A is cut out in the centre to create a frame – you will need to use a scalpel or craft knife for this step.

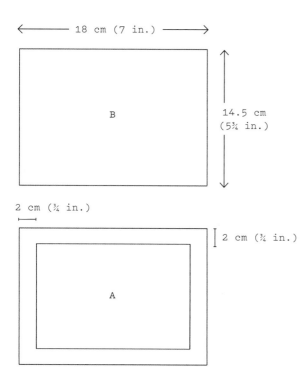

2 The four scenic panels of the peepshow 'book' are cut from mid-weight (160 gsm) paper. If you are using the Layer 1-4 scenic templates provided on pp.86-87, enlarge and transfer the designs to your paper (see p.19 for instructions). Cut them out, score along the dashed fold lines, then fold back to form tabs. Transfer and cut out the moon design on the Back template to your back piece B. Decorate the scenic panels as you wish, with paints, pens or crayons, or leave blank.

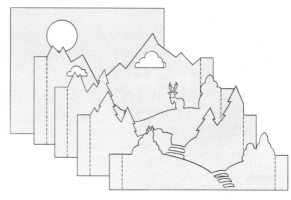

3 If you would prefer to use your own found imagery to create your scenic panels, first make the bases. Cut four strips from mid-weight (160 gsm) paper, each 2 cm x 21 cm (¾ x 8¼ in.). On each strip, measure 1.5 cm (⅝ in.) in from both sides, score fold lines and fold back the edges to form tabs (these will eventually be used to glue the panels in place).

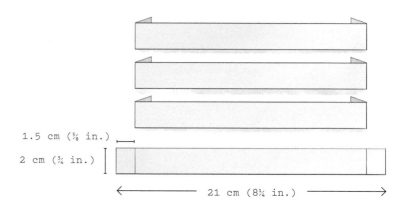

Print your chosen images directly onto mid-weight (160 gsm) paper or cut out pictures from magazines, backing them before attaching to the strips.

4 To decorate your panels, first decide on your theme or imagery – trees, in our example – and decide what will be on each of the four panels and the back panel B. As the peepshow extends, a 'depth of field' is created, so select something simple (for example a sun, moon or clouds) for the back panel B. The scenes should gradually decrease in height and increase in detail as you get nearer to the 'foreground'. With this in mind, attach your images to panel B and to the base strips. Print your images direct to mid-weight (160 gsm) paper, cut them out (using a scalpel or craft scissors), and glue them to the strips. Alternatively, cut images roughly from magazines or similar and back them onto this paper before cutting out the details.

5 Cut two pieces of mid-weight (160 gsm) paper, each measuring 14.5 x 20 cm (5¾ x 7⅞ in.). Using a ruler and pencil, mark the long edge of each strip in 2 cm (¾ in.) increments, then score and fold to create two concertina-folded side pieces.

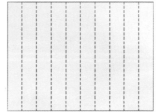

6 Starting with one of the concertina side pieces, glue the scenic panels in place, in order, as shown in the illustration below (note the position of the front-most panel, inside the first concertina fold). Once all panels have been glued to the first side piece, attach the other tabs to the second concertina piece in the same way, ensuring both sides match up. **Tip:** *Apply glue to the panel tabs using a glue brush and a stippling motion, to achieve a thin, even coat. You can ensure good adhesion by placing waste paper over each glued join and smoothing it flat for a few minutes using your fingers or a bone folder.*

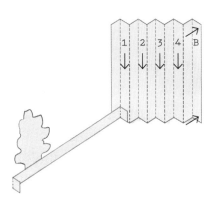

7 Finish by gluing panel A, the frame, to the front. This forms a viewing window and strengthens the entire structure. **Tip:** *Once everything is glued together, place the folded peepshow between heavy books or boards for 20-30 minutes to make sure everything dries flat.*

8 The final step is making the wrap-around cover. Start by measuring the full width (closed) depth, and height of your book so far. (The width should be 18 cm (7 in.) and the height should be 14.5 cm (5¾ in.) but the depth may vary.) Using these measurements, mark up your heavyweight (200 gsm) paper or thin card according to the diagram below. Cut this template out, score along the dashed lines and fold.

9 To create a viewing window in the cover, as shown in the diagram, carefully mark the centre of the 'front' cover flap (it can be either) and use a circle cutter to make this aperture. Alternatively, draw around a circular object and cut out the shape with a craft knife. Fold in the cover flaps, mark the same circle on the second flap, so they match up, and cut again.

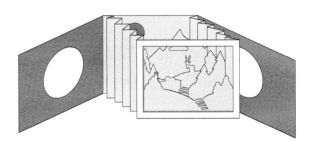

Three times the width and twice the depth of finished book

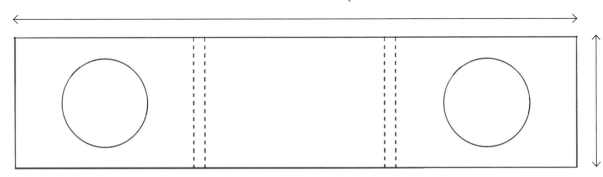

If you are adding a viewing window, make sure each one lines up
when the book cover is closed.

10 The back panel of your peepshow can
now be glued to the centre panel of the
cover or, alternatively, keep the cover
loose, so the peepshow itself can be
removed. This can work well if your scenic
panels have holes cut into them — a light
source behind will add to the drama of
your finished book.

Now try...

Something a bit more complex. You can add to
the number of folds in the side panels, and add
extra layers – some nineteenth-century examples
have ten or more scenes! It is also possible to
create sophisticated effects using copies of the
same image for each 'panel'; the image (a map,
for instance) can be used in full at the back of
the book, with the layers in front increasingly
cut away, to create a 3D effect.

Scenic templates

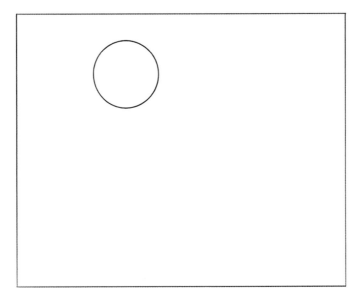

Back

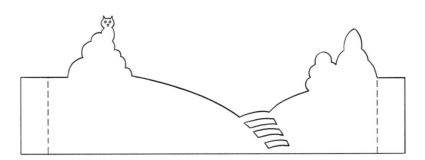

Layer 1

Templates shown at 50%

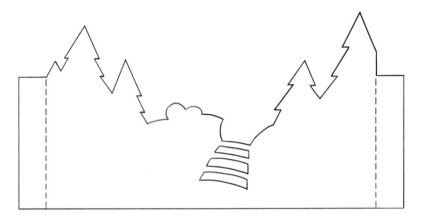

Layer 2

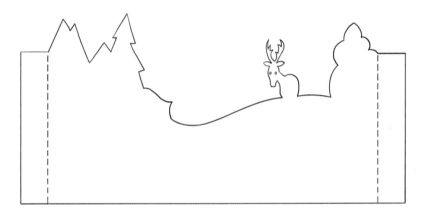

Layer 3

Layer 4

STICKING

We're surrounded by paper in daily life, much of it intended to be throwaway. With sticking, paper's seemingly fragile ephemerality becomes permanent and durable. Paper modelling fixes it into forms for preservation, while making a collage or work of découpage encourages us to look again at what might otherwise be discarded. Seeking out colours, patterns and images to cut out and repurpose can reveal the potential of even the most mundane materials.

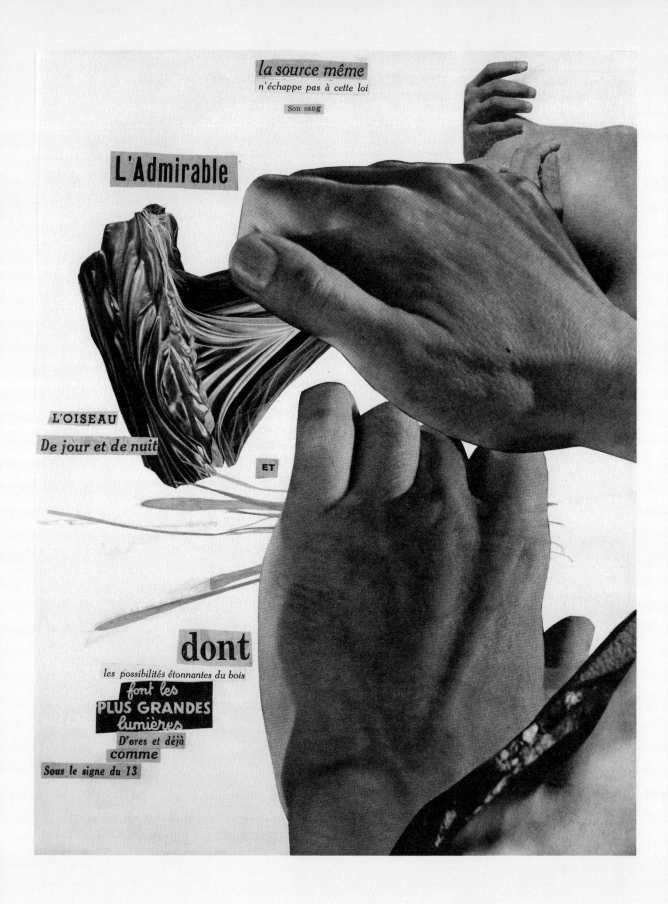

la source même
n'échappe pas à cette loi

Son sang

L'Admirable

L'OISEAU

De jour et de nuit

ET

dont

les possibilités étonnantes du bois

font les
PLUS GRANDES
lumières

D'ores et déjà
comme

Sous le signe du 13

Paper crafts based on sticking draw on the techniques of papercutting, folding and forming, but they also have their own distinctive creative tradition. While their popularity is more recent than that of other crafts, there are surprising historical precedents. For example, interest in découpage – decorating surfaces by pasting on paper cut-outs – can be traced back to sixteenth-century manuscripts in the Ottoman court, while quilling – the rolling and shaping of strips or ribbons of paper into elaborate patterns, also known as filigree or rolled paperwork – was used in fifteenth-century English churches in place of expensive metal filigree decoration.

However, the height of both these decorative techniques was in Europe from the eighteenth century. The enthusiasm with which Parisian society embraced découpage is captured in a 1727 letter from Mademoiselle Charlotte Aïssé to her friend Madame Calandrini in Geneva: 'Every lady, great and small, is cutting away ... We make wall panels, screens and firebirds of them. There are books and engravings that cost up to 100 lire, and women are mad enough to cut up engravings worth 100 lire apiece. If this fashion continues, they will cut up Raphaels!' Unsurprisingly,

businesses began catering to this new pastime, printing 'scraps' specifically for découpage. Inspiration could be found from plenty of sources: the English poet Lord Byron used images of boxing and other amusements from books and periodicals to découpage a two-metre-tall screen.

'Paper models' were also produced – printed designs, to be cut out, assembled and stuck together; mainly educational in purpose, the models ranged from landmarks to farmhouses – while quillers' needs were also well furnished. Between 1780 and 1830, the period in which rolled paperwork was at its most fashionable, plain boxes with raised surfaces were sold especially for the purpose (see p.94 for more details), along with strips of coloured paper, often with gilt edges, and sheets of designs.

Although cutting and sticking to create new images had been practised for centuries, it was the Cubists who elevated collage into an art form in the early twentieth century. When French artist Georges Braque incorporated a typeset phrase into his 1911 painting, *The Portuguese*, he argued it was 'to get as close as I could to reality'. Pushing the conventions of

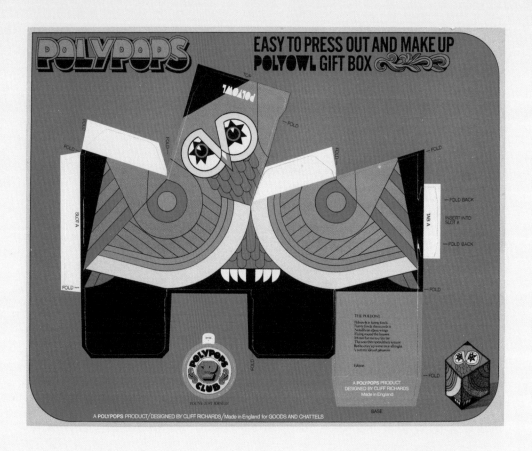

painting, this work engaged with the visual material
of the modern world.

Following Braque's experiments, collage – from
the French 'coller', 'to stick', and meaning the pasting
of pre-existing materials onto a two-dimensional
surface – inspired many different artistic movements.
The 'poèmes-découpages' of French Surrealist Georges
Hugnet's 1936 La Septième Face du dé (The Seventh
Face of the Dice) feature 'ready-made' words cut from
periodicals and arranged around photomontages,
embracing the unusual, unsettling contrasts created.

While Pop Art collages questioned consumer culture
in the 1960s, paper's potential was also being explored
by product designers. Polypops Products' colourful
and playful children's range included Clifford Richards'
'The Polyowl' of 1968, which – when cut out from its
card and assembled using the foldable tabs – formed
an owl-shaped gift box. This company had grown out of
the development of a more ambitious form of folding
and sticking: cardboard furniture. American Home

extolled such furniture's 'inexpensive, decorative, gay,
immediately available and easily disposable' virtues.
British designer Peter Murdoch's 'Chair Thing', a child's
chair made from a single sheet of folded card, sold
around 76,000 pieces over a six-month period in 1967.

Smaller-scale paper modelling also continued,
its popularity reflected by the Victoria and Albert
Museum's Robert Freidus Architectural Paper Model
Collection: over 14,000 paper architectural models of
varying complexity, gathered from over forty different
countries (see p.110). That tradition is embraced today
by the likes of Canadian 'paper engineer' Yee Job – who
sells paper-kit Sydney Opera House and Osaka Castle
models and has even created a paper V12 engine with
moveable crankshaft, rods and pistons – as well as
the 'custom paper craft sculpture atelier' of Deniz &
Türker Akman. Working together as Papier Atelier, this
Istanbul-based duo conceive cut-fold-and-stick models
that prove paper can be used to create anything from
polar bears to portraits.

Left: Nursery screen,
late 19th century
Paper collage on
canvas on wood

QUILLING

Tea caddy, 1800–20

Rolled paperwork, also known as quilling or filigree work, has been used as a decorative technique for centuries. By the eighteenth century, it was considered a suitable pursuit for ladies and, being small and light, tea caddies such as this one were ideal canvases for this kind of decoration. The serving of tea had itself become a genteel social event. Wooden caddies with raised edges, leaving recessed panels, were made by specialist box makers specifically to be decorated with tightly rolled strips of brightly coloured and gilded paper. Boxes containing pre-cut papers and printed sheets of designs (see below) could also be purchased from specialist shops. Even so, a caddy like this would have taken hours of painstaking work to complete, before being displayed along with other fine accessories on the tea table.

Rolled paperwork on a wooden frame, with brass handle
Great Britain, 14 x 20 x 12 cm (5½ x 8 x 4¾ in.)
V&A: W.73–1981

Bemrose & Son Ltd, Mosaicon,
1870-90, Great Britain
Kit for making filigree paperwork.
The box contains packets of
strips of paper, loose strips
of paper, short lengths of wood
for rolling the paper, and sheets
of instruction and advertising.
V&A: W.40-1934
Given by Miss Ethel A. G. Willoughby

FRAMED QUILLED MOTIF

This vibrant decorative piece takes its design cues from a nineteenth-century tea caddy, decorated in only slightly less bold tones by its owner (see pp.94–95). A quilling tool is required, as well as some patience and delicacy, but don't be put off by the seeming intricacy of the work. Once you have practised working a few shapes, the construction of the design is relatively simple.

Project by Sena Runa

You will need

2 sheets white lightweight (90 gsm) paper, min 25 x 25 cm (10 x 10 in.)
Cork board
Pins
151 strips of lightweight (80-120 gsm) craft paper, each 1 cm (⅜ in.) in width. **Note:** *These can be bought pre-cut or you can simply cut larger sheets of paper to size using a cutting mat and craft knife or scalpel, as follows:* 16 x dark blue (max. 30 cm/12 in.) 16 x mid blue (9 cm/3½ in.) 3 x light blue (9 cm/3½ in.) 27 x teal (max. 30 cm/12 in.) 4 x purple (max. 30 cm/12 in.) 30 x violet (max. 30 cm/12 in.) 37 x yellow (max. 30 cm/12 in.) 6 x orange (max. 23 cm/9 in.) 5 x pink (max. 30 cm/12 in.) 7 x light green (max. 30 cm/12 in.)
Quilling tool: either a slotted tool or quilling needle
Circle ruler/template
Craft scissors
PVA glue with fine applicator
Tweezers
White box frame, approx. 25 x 25 x 4 cm (10 x 10 x 2 in.)

Optional (if you are cutting your own paper strips)
Cutting mat
Metal ruler
Craft knife or scalpel, with blades

How to make

1 Photocopy or otherwise transfer the design template on p.102 to a sheet of white paper. Attach the template to the cork board using pins positioned in each corner of the sheet.

2 Prepare a diamond shape using a mid-blue strip cut to 9 cm (3½ in.) in length. Thread the very end of the strip into a slotted quilling tool or simply begin to wind a coil around a quilling needle. Coil the entire strip tightly around the tool and then remove.

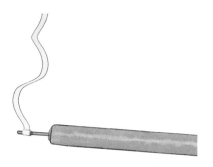

3 Allow the coil to unwind or loosen slightly before securing the end of the paper strip with a dab of glue.

4 Then, using your fingertips, compress two opposite sides of the coil to form a marquise or 'eye' shape. Do the same to the other sides, creating a diamond. Repeat to make six diamonds in total – three mid blue and three light blue.
Tip: *Make sure all six shapes are the same size and fit the diamond shape in the printed template. A circle ruler/ template (see photograph opposite) can be useful but it may still take a bit of trial end error to get this right. Practise on scrap paper if you need to.*

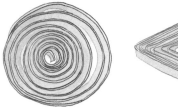
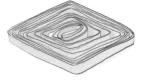

5 Glue the six diamonds to each other, alternating the colours. Use tiny dabs of PVA glue to form the flower shape at the centre of the design template. Do not attach the shapes directly to your template sheet (which is simply used for placement), but position and hold them in place using pins through the white paper and cork board.

6 Cut a teal strip to 30 cm (12 in.) in length and curl it using scissors, by carefully pulling the paper over the blunt edge of the blade. Position this paper strip on the template, creating a circle that hugs tightly around the central flower shape and sticking the end of the curled strip in place to hold the circle in position. Using dabs of glue at the tips of the diamond 'petals' will also help to secure this circle. As before, do not stick the paper down to the template.
Tip: *Tweezers will help you to hold and manipulate the paper without misshaping it or spreading glue everywhere.*

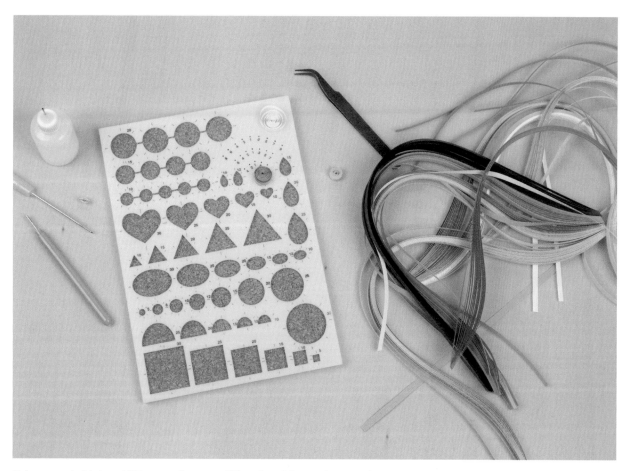

Using specialist quilling equipment will make this project easier. From left to right: quilling tools, shape template and pre-cut paper strips.

7 Make six tight quilled circular coils using teal strips cut to 3.5 cm (1⅜ in.); secure the ends of the paper with glue. Position these inside the teal circle in such a way that they fill the gaps between the diamond-shape petals of the flower. Again, ensure these coils are the same size using a circular ruler, if you have one.

8 Take four purple strips, each 30 cm (12 in.) long, and roll them around the teal circle tightly without leaving any gap. It will help to curl the paper strips first, as you did before, and move them using tweezers. Use dabs of glue to secure the ends of each strip.

9 Take five violet strips, each 30 cm (12 in. long) and roll them tightly around the outside of the purple circle, following the same procedure as that set out in the previous step.

10 Using strips measuring 23 cm (9 in.) in length, make twelve tight coils – six yellow and six orange – and glue these to the outside of the violet circle, alternating yellow and orange coils as shown in the photograph on p.97.

11 Apply a dot of glue to the outside of each of the yellow and orange coils. Take five pink strips, each 30 cm (12 in.) long, and roll them tightly around the outside, fixing the ends in place with a dab of glue, observing the design template underneath. As before, use pins through the template sheet and cork board to hold each element in place while you are working.

12 Make twenty violet diamond shapes using strips 14 cm (5½ in.) long. Glue these to the outside of the dark-pink circle you have just made, so that they run around the design, again using dots of glue applied to the smaller shapes.

13 Take five violet strips, each 30 cm (12 in.) long, and roll them tightly around the outside of the layer of diamond shapes to create a new circle, securing the strips with glue.

14 Take twenty teal strips, each 30 cm (12 in.) long, and roll them around the purple circle. Around the outside of this, roll seven light-green strips, each 30 cm (12 in.) long.

15 Using strips measuring 30 cm (12 in.) in length, make twenty-six tight coils – thirteen mid blue and thirteen dark blue – and glue these to the outside of the last, light-green circle, alternating mid blue and dark blue.

16 Take three dark-blue strips, each 30 cm (12 in.) long, and place around the layer of blue coils to make a circle, observing the design template underneath. Around the outside of this, roll three yellow strips, each 30 cm (12 in.) long, as before.

17 Using fourteen yellow strips cut to 3.5 cm (1⅜ in.) in length, make fourteen semi-circles. The strips are simply curled over scissors, and then glued to the previous yellow layer in semi-circle shapes, secured at each end of the strip by a small dab of glue, as shown in the photograph opposite.

18 Using strips measuring 15 cm (6 in.) in length, make fourteen tight yellow coils. Position these, one inside each yellow semi-circle, and glue in place using small dabs of glue applied to the outside edges of each coil.

Adding pink and violet heart shapes is the final step.

19 Make fourteen heart scrolls – seven pink and seven violet – using strips measuring 30 cm (12 in.) in length. To make the heart shapes, fold each strip in half and roll loose coils inwards from each end of the strip. These two coils are then released and glued together to form the heart. Position these between the semi-circle shapes and glue in place.

20 Your artwork is now ready to frame. Remove the pins and carefully lift the quilled design from the template sheet. Glue it in place on your second sheet of white paper. Trim this sheet to size and position within your box frame, gluing or taping the white backing to the back of the frame if necessary, to make sure it stays in position.

Now try...

Different designs. You can use the basic quilled shapes from this project (and others – there are lots of online tutorials showing how to create different quilled shapes) to create any design you can think up. We have supplied two extra templates on p.103 for you to try, but you can also improvise and design your own!

Design template

Templates shown at 100%

DÉCOUPAGE

Wallpaper, 1725–75

Découpage – from the French *découper* (meaning 'to cut out')
– is the art of decorating surfaces or objects with paper cut-
outs. The practice has a long lineage – Siberian nomads before
Christ's birth decorated objects with cut-out felt figures – and
has attracted varying definitions over its long, complex history.
The term is nowadays often associated with the practice of
pasting cut-out paper images onto objects and then layering
varnish over the top, achieving a shiny, flat lacquered effect
(see project overleaf).

Chinese wallpapers – fashionable in large European
houses in the eighteenth century – often had cut-out paper
birds and flowers added to the scheme after they were hung.
For instance, at Temple Newsam in West Yorkshire, England,
in the late 1820s, Lady Hertford stuck to the wallpaper birds
cut out not only from unused parts of the paper itself, but also
from a copy of J.J. Audubon's *Birds of America* (1838), making
the design unique to her home.

Ink and watercolour on paper, China, 279 x 164 cm (110 x 64½ in.)
V&A: E.2083–1914. Given by HM Commissioners of Woods, Forest
and Land Revenues

DÉCOUPAGE WOODEN TRAY

This project combines découpage with simple papercutting – this is a small and accessible piece of design, using a simple wooden tray. You could, however, apply the same techniques to a photo-frame, mirror, chair or any other item you would like to customize; the finished effect is determined by your own choice of imagery and theme. Victorian paper vignettes and ephemera, like those shown here, can be found at vintage and specialist fairs, or in copyright-free books and collections.

Project by Florrie Thomas

You will need

1 wooden tray (preferably with an untreated surface)

Selection of printed images for découpage

Craft scissors

1 sheet A4 mid-weight white craft paper, max. 160 gsm

Cutting mat

Scalpel with blades

Ruler

Pencil

Spray mount and/or PVA glue

Quick-drying matt, clear, wood varnish and brush

Optional

Lightweight copy paper, at least 90 gsm (unless using already-printed media)

Desktop printer or colour photocopier

How to make

1 Clean and dry the wooden tray to ensure glue adheres well to the surface.

2 Gather your images: collect together printed media, or print or photocopy your image selection to copy paper. Cut out all the images with scissors.

3 Transfer the design template on p.109 onto your craft paper (see p.19 for full instructions).

4 Use your scalpel and cutting mat to cut out the scalloped design, starting by cutting out the middle of the shape.

5 Find the central point of your tray using a ruler and place the papercut design over it. This provides a focal point for the design and will help you to structure your image placement. Start to place the cut-out images around the tray, playing with different layouts. Work outwards from the papercut, placing images in and around it and experimenting with overlapping images. **Tip:** *Try a few options before committing to a layout.*

6 Take a photograph of your layout, in case you need to refer back to it as you move images around. Stick the images in place, overlapping where necessary. Spray mount will give a flat and even coating of glue (PVA is useful for pre-assembling overlapping images, which can be attached to the tray as a unit). Once all the pieces are stuck in place, allow to dry.

7 Apply at least four coats of varnish over the whole surface, following the manufacturer's instructions and allowing each coat to dry completely. The varnish transforms a fragile piece of paper into an integral part of the wooden tray. **Note:** *Do not use strong cleaning products or immerse the tray in water, as you may damage the découpage.*

Play around with image placement before you stick anything down. Use the papercut border to anchor your design.

Now try...

Découpage with papercuts. While there are lots of different kinds of printed media available – wrapping paper, wallpaper, old maps, stamps and postcards, to name just a few – you can découpage using only your own original papercuts. Take a look at some of the other projects in this book (see pp.54, 64 and 72) for inspiration.

Design template

Template shown at 100%

PAPER MODELLING

Kleine Bahnbauten ('Small Railway Buildings'), 2002

The first paper models designed to be cut out from a printed sheet and assembled appeared in Europe in the 1600s, and commercial versions were included in French toy catalogues in 1800. Their popularity surged in the nineteenth century and endures into the present.

Produced by German company Stipp, this paper model kit contains two sheets of paper with detailed assembly instructions and one sheet of card with realistically rendered and coloured cut-out models of eleven small railway buildings, including a tool shed, phone cabins, toilets, station house plus various outbuildings. As is traditional in German toys, all aspects of the technical buildings that were present on the railway lines at that time are depicted in minute detail. Each building is rendered with perfectly articulated materials and surfaces such as wood, metal and bricks, which are worn and weathered by the elements and time with creeping plants and even broken windows. There are also additional doors and windows that can be added to make the buildings more three-dimensional. The only other elements needed to construct the models are patience, scissors and glue.

Coloured printed card, Germany, 33 x 21.5 cm (13 x 8½ in.)
V&A: B.401:1 to 3-2015
Part of the Robert Freidus Architectural Paper Model Collection

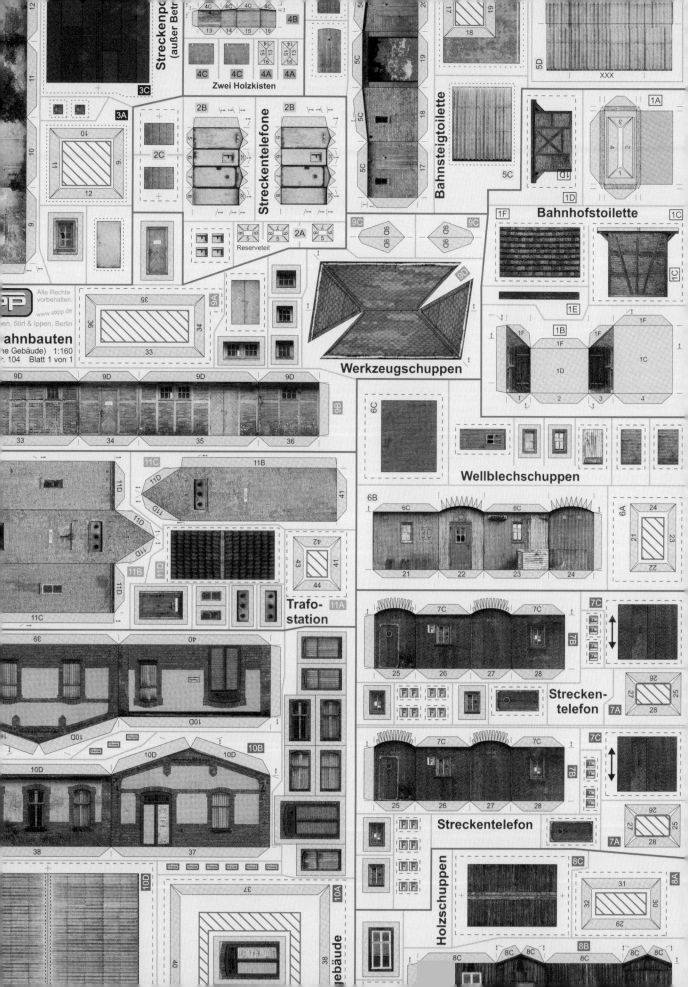

MODEL VILLAGE

Paper models – produced on a sheet of paper, to be cut out and assembled – have given their owners a glimpse of places in distant parts of the world since the seventeenth century. With the advent of mass printing, such models became even more popular, representing both famous and archetypical buildings and living spaces. The three templates provided here, when 'built', form a small hamlet of three houses. Using flameless lights, they can be turned into a charming, illuminated winter village.

Project by Julianna Szabo

You will need

8 sheets of A4 lightweight white copy paper, 80 gsm, or tracing paper
8 sheets of A4 mid-weight white card, 270 gsm
Craft knife/scalpel with blades
Masking tape
Cutting mat
Metal ruler
Scoring tool
Pencil
Bone folder
Paper glue/all-purpose glue (not PVA)

Opposite: House 1 (centre), House 2 (right), House 3 (left).

How to make

Score along the dashed lines before cutting out the pieces.

1 Photocopy or otherwise transfer the house templates on pp.117-23 (see p.19 for full instructions) to white copy paper or tracing paper. **Note:** *For each house, there are two types of roof-tile template. Consult the printed templates for notes on how many to cut and trace the relevant template the required number of times.*

2 Using a craft knife or scalpel, roughly cut around each of the templates, leaving approx. 1 cm (½ in.) around the outlines.

3 Working on one house at a time, use small strips of masking tape to secure the templates to your white card. Place a strip every 2-3 cm (¾-1⅛ in.) around the template edges, to make sure the template will not move on the card when you are scoring and cutting.

4 Working on a cutting mat, and using the scoring tool and a metal ruler, score along all the dashed lines on each template. Push the scorer hard enough to leave a mark on the card, but be careful not to push too hard, or you will go through your template. **Tip:** *If you don't have a scorer, you can also use an empty ballpoint pen.*

5 Cut out all the windows and doors before cutting along the house template outlines, using a craft knife or scalpel and a metal ruler. Cut using continuous lines. (At this stage, your paper templates will come away from the card and can be put to one side.)

For House 1 and House 2

1 The scored side of the card will be the inside of the house. Fold along all scored edges, folding towards the scored side except along those two lines that are shown in red on the template – these should be folded away from the scored side of the house (and will eventually make the roof eaves). Use a bone folder to ensure nice, crisp folds.

2 Apply glue to the outer side of the tab marked 1 on house part 1. Align the fold of the tab with the edge marked 1 on house part 2, making sure part 2 is under part 1, so the tab will end up inside the finished building. Press the two parts together firmly and hold until the glue sets.
Tip: *Use your little finger to spread glue evenly on the tabs – you will use that finger the least when working, so you won't smear glue where it doesn't belong. Make sure you apply glue evenly all over the relevant tabs and wait for the glue to set after sticking before moving on to the next step.*

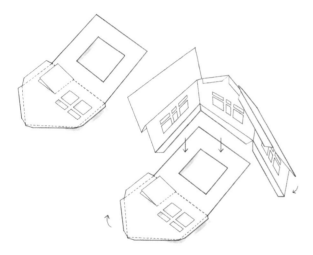

3 To form the eaves, spread glue on the area between the top of the wall and the roof (marked grey on the template). Fold the roof down over this area, press the two together, and hold until the glue is properly set. Complete this step on both sides of the house.

4 Glue the base of the house to the tabs on the bottom of the side walls. Next, glue the front of the house to the side walls – make sure you put glue on the outside of the relevant tabs, so that the tabs themselves end up inside the house.

5 Next, glue the side of the roof with the tab on top to the tabs of the front and back walls, aligning the wall tabs with the ends of the roof tab to create eaves (the roof is slightly wider than the house).

6 Apply glue to the remaining tabs and gently attach the other roof half to them, aligning the two roofs at the top. If necessary, you can push the tabs outwards to meet the roof, using the bone folder, from the bottom of the house.

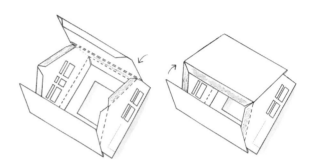

7 To form the tiled roof, take a chipped tile strip from the set of 12 for House 1 (or 17, for House 2) and spread glue on it. Position the strip on the roof, aligning the inner tips of the chipped side with the bottom edge of the roof. Continue to glue on tile strips, always aligning the chip tips with the top of the previous strip, creating a tiny overlap between tiles, until you reach the top of the roof. Repeat on the other side. **Note:** *On House 2, there will be 7 strips on the short side, and 10 on the long side of the roof.*

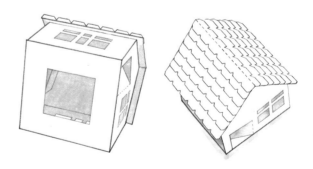

8 To finish the house, put glue on the top tile strip (the one chipped on both sides) and attach it to the roof apex.

For House 3

1 The scored side of the card pieces will be the 'inside' of the house. Fold along all scored lines as per the instructions in step 1 above (Houses 1 and 2), taking special care with the lines marked red.

2 As per steps 2-4 above (Houses 1 and 2), attach parts 1 and 2 of the house using the tab marked 1, then form the roof eaves and assemble the main part of the house using the tabs on the side walls.

3 When both side walls are glued to the front of the house, glue the roof to the side and back walls using the tabs.

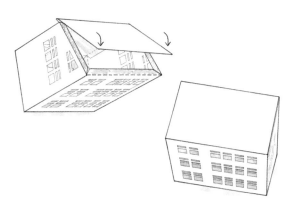

4 Assemble the house extension and garage building. **Note:** *The extension has no back wall, only tabs at the reverse and this means the order of assembly is not so important as for the main house, as all tabs should remain easy to access no matter in what order they are glued. The garage is a smaller version of the main building and can be glued together in a similar order (see steps 3 and 4 for Houses 1 and 2).*

5 Glue the extension and garage to the main building. Apply glue to all of the tabs on the reverse of the extension and press it firmly to the front-left side of the main building in one motion. Likewise, apply glue to the back wall of the garage and press it firmly to the right side of the main building, holding in place until the glue sets.

6 To form the tiled roof of the main building, take a chipped tile strip from the set of 10 longer strips and spread glue on it. Position the strip on the roof, aligning the inner tips of the chipped side with the bottom edge of the roof. Continue to glue on tile strips, always aligning the chip tips with the top of the previous strip, creating a tiny overlap between tiles, until you reach the top of the roof.

7 To finish the house, put glue on the top tile strip (the one chipped on both sides) and attach it to the roof apex.

8 Repeat steps 6 and 7 using the shorter tile strips on the garage roof.

Now try...

Lighting up the town! The houses are each designed with a hole in the base panels, so that you can put a flameless light inside each one and turn the little hamlet into a glowing display. You can also try using coloured card or changing the shape of the doors and windows, to alter the character of your little hamlet.

Templates for House 1

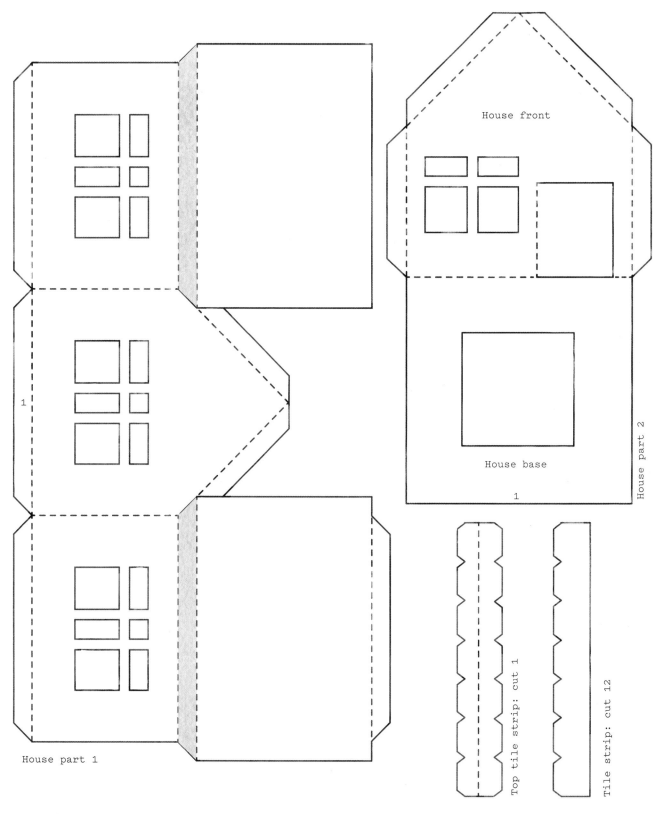

House front

House base

House part 2

1

House part 1

Top tile strip: cut 1

Tile strip: cut 12

Templates shown at 100%

Templates for House 2

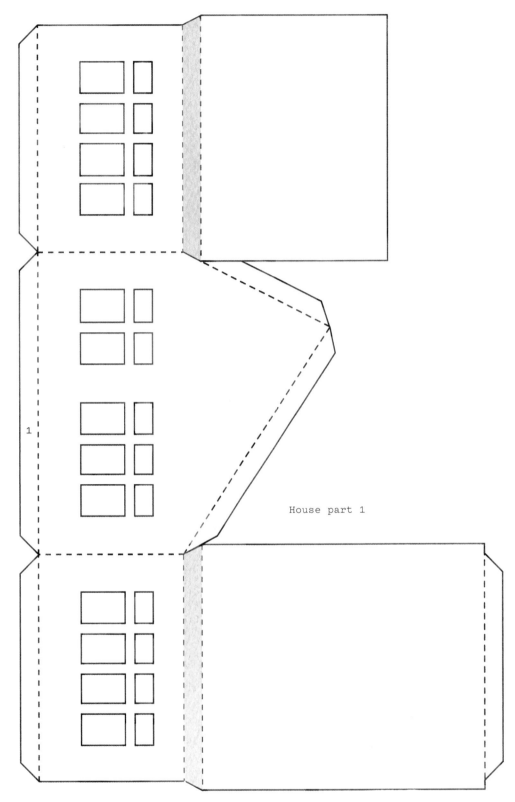

1

House part 1

Templates shown at 100%

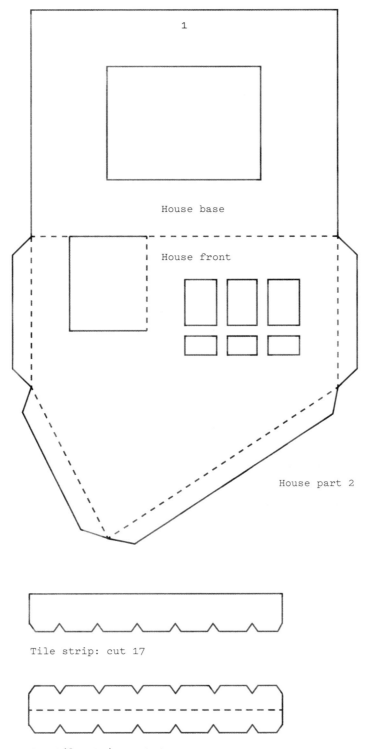

1

House base

House front

House part 2

Tile strip: cut 17

Top tile strip: cut 1

Templates shown at 100%

Templates for House 3

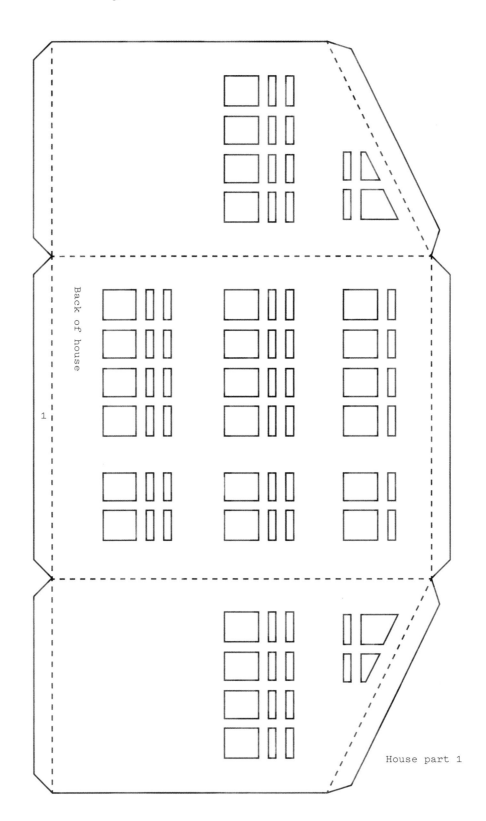

Back of house

1

House part 1

Templates shown at 100%

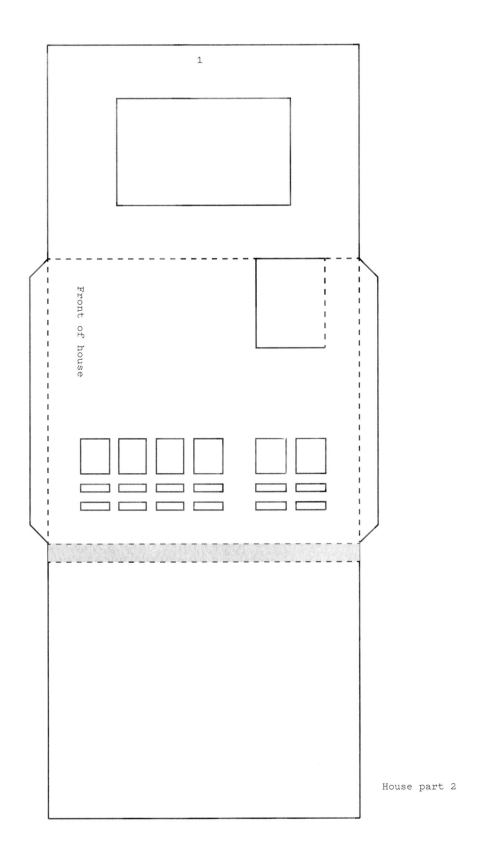

1

Front of house

House part 2

Templates shown at 100%

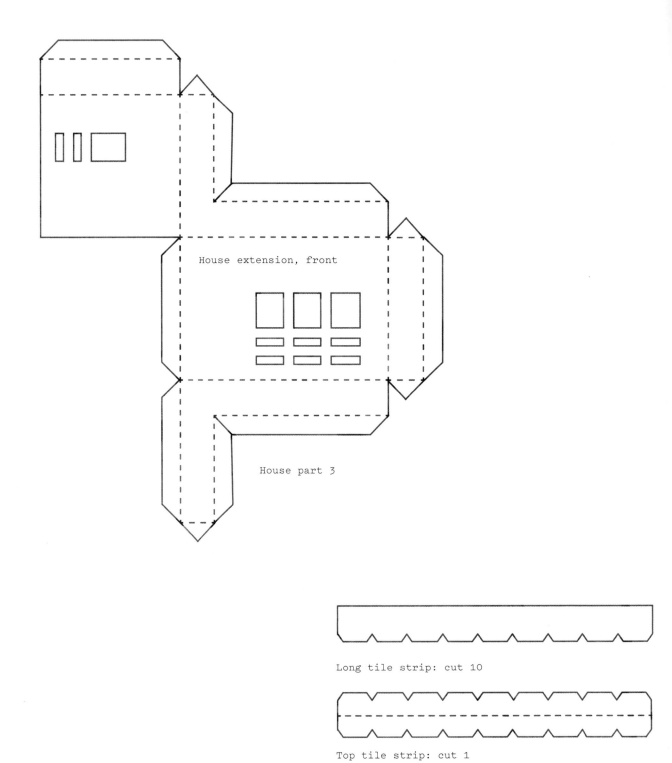

House extension, front

House part 3

Long tile strip: cut 10

Top tile strip: cut 1

Short tile strip: cut 6

Templates shown at 100%

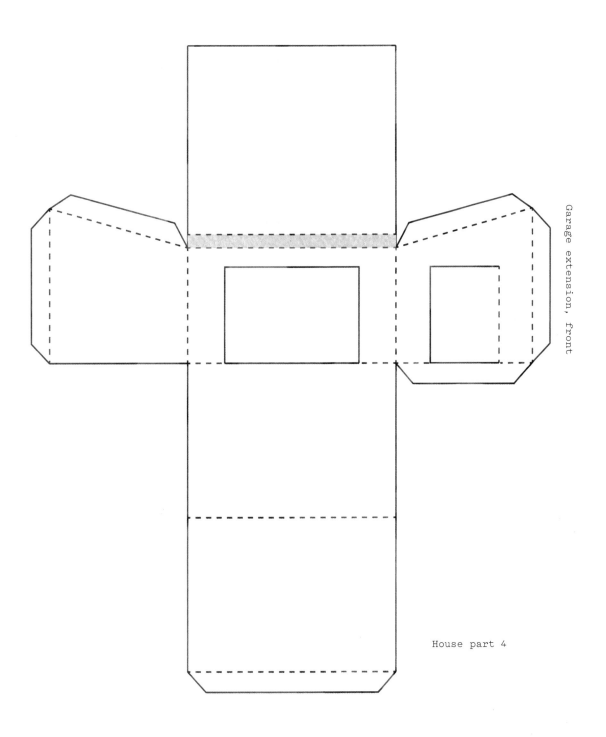

Garage extension, front

House part 4

Templates shown at 100%

FORMING

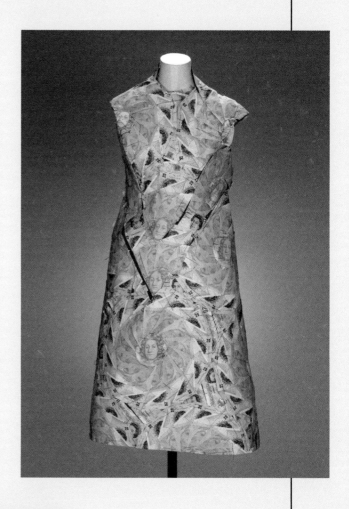

Facing page, top: Russell Sage,
dress, 2001, Great Britain
Paper, length: 110.5 cm (43½ in.)
V&A: T.391-2001
Given by Britannic Money plc

Facing page, bottom: Pen box,
c. 1865, Kashmir
Papier mâché, 28.5 x 5.5 x 6.5 cm
(11¼ x 2 x 2¼ in.)
V&A: 02343(IS)

Right: Papier-mâché bust of a woman,
16th century, Italy

Below: Piñatas hanging on strings
of lights in Cozumel, Mexico, 2010

We take paper so much for granted that it's easy to forget that
every sheet is a wonder of technology, the result of a process
that's been refined over centuries. But a sheet isn't the only
form paper has to take – it can be broken back down into its pulp
and remoulded, sewn, plaited, woven and even worn. Hands-on
experimentation is a way to rediscover paper's possibilities as
a material, perhaps even inspiring ways of creative reinvention.

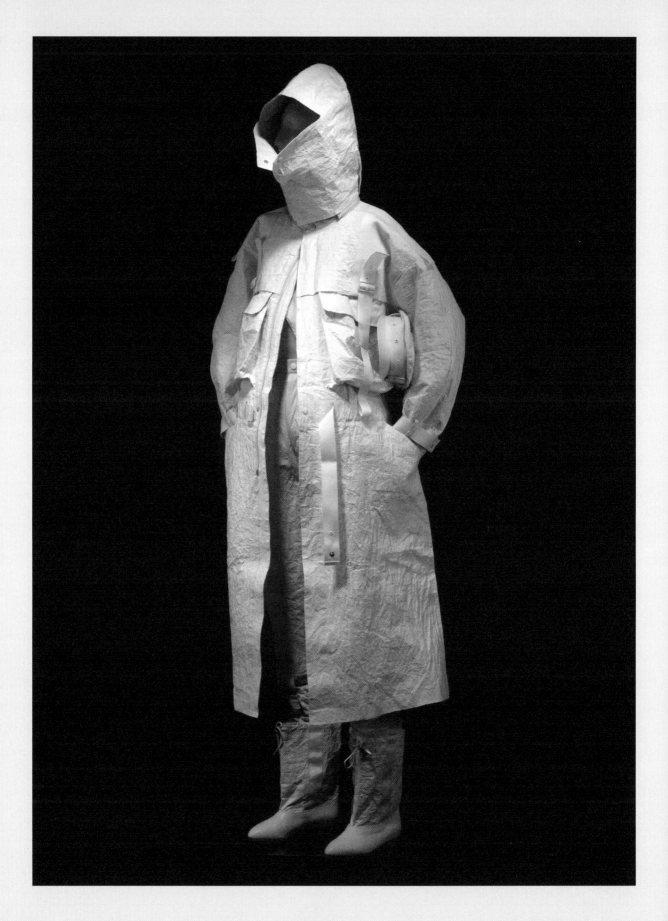

Facing page: Issey Miyake, cap, hood,
jacket, trousers and boots, 1983,
Japan
Kozo paper with assorted materials,
various dimensions
V&A: FE.30B-F-1983

The earliest examples of paper are found in China. Not the work of Cai Lun, who was recorded as paper's inventor in AD 105, but in the form of a map, dating to 65 BC, and a letter-like fragment from 8 BC, discovered in Dunhuang in 2006. This find included more than 30,000 paper rolls, preserved thanks to the dry climate and encompassing religious, government and business documents, as well as paper flowers. Made from layers of coloured and inked paper and dating to between the seventh and tenth centuries, these paper flowers were probably Buddhist votive offerings, an example of one of many paper-flower folk art traditions found around the world, from Mexico to Japan.

Although he didn't invent paper, it's probable that Cai Lun improved it. Using tree bark – from mulberry, paper mulberry and sandalwood trees – with hemp, cloth rags and fishing nets, was less expensive than the production of the silk paper or bamboo tablets previously used. China's paper-making techniques spread to Japan and Korea (a set of contemporary vases in the V&A use the traditional Korean *hanji* paper, made with mulberry bark; see p.162) and, via the Silk Road overland trade route, to the Islamic world, and from there, Europe. The process of making paper by hand (as it was in China until the nineteenth century) is illustrated in Song Yingxing's 1643 *Tiangong Kaiwu* ('The Exploitation of the Works of Nature'), which shows each stage, from the gathering and preparation of bamboo stalks to sheets being hung outside to dry. Today, hand-making paper can be explored as an art form, as seen in Angela Lorenz's work (see p.130).

The intrinsic qualities of paper have inspired their own craft traditions. Distinct from the manipulation of a sheet of paper, these techniques are used to create three-dimensional, sculptural objects. Although the term papier mâché (French for 'mashed paper') dates to eighteenth-century England, this technique probably also originated in East Asia. From the fifteenth century, pulp composed of paper, mixed with other fibrous materials and bound with an adhesive, was associated with makers in India (especially the city of Srinagar), whose mastery of the material was applied to the likes of delicate trays, cigar boxes and candlesticks for export to Europe.

Within Europe, papier mâché was used to create objects ranging from picture frames to sculpture; snuff boxes to architectural ornaments. A commercial

Above: Nel Linssen, bracelet, 1986, Netherlands
Pleated paper and elastic, height: 4.6 cm (1¾ in.)
V&A: M.38-2014. The Louise Klapisch Collection,
given by Suzanne Selvi

Left: Wastebasket Boutique by Mars,
paper dress, 1967, USA
Printed and bonded cellulose fibre,
length: 90.5 cm (35½ in.)
V&A: T.32-1992. Bequeathed by Audie Bancroft

Facing page, top: Ellen Bell,
The Journeyman, 2001, Great Britain
Magazine ephemera, sewn paper
and wire hanger, 76 x 71.5 x 6 cm
(30 x 28 x 2½ in.)
V&A: E.1094-2002. Purchased through
the Julie and Robert Breckman
Print Fund

Facing page, bottom: Tokujin
Yoshioka, Honey-Pop Chair, 2005
(designed 2001), Japan
Concertina-folded paper,
partially unfolded and crushed
by body of designer, 83 x 77 x 80 cm
(32½ x 30¼ x 31½ in.)
V&A: W.5-2005. Given by the designer

recipe, producing an effect similar to that of East Asian lacquered work, was patented in 1772. This so-called 'japanning' was used to create beautiful decorative objects, usually in red, green or black, gilded, finely painted and highly polished. Between 1840 and 1860, when its popularity was at its height, papier mâché was even used for larger functional items such as chairs.

In contrast, papier-mâché objects from Mexico have deliberately short lifespans. 'Judas' figures, in the form of devils, skeletons or perhaps contemporary personalities, are made for Easter, to be burned or filled with fireworks and exploded. Paper pulp is also used to create skeletal Day of the Dead figures, and animal, bird and reptile masks for festivities. This heritage may have inspired the giant papier-mâché puppets often seen at anti-globalization protests. The piñata, a feature at many different celebrations in an array of inventive shapes, is often formed from a hollow shell of papier mâché that is filled with sweets and gifts, under decoration made from layers of coloured paper strips. The piñata is hit with a stick and, once broken, the sweets spill out.

Many designers and makers today are exploring paper's potential to form new objects. The Dutch jeweller Nel Linssen creates elaborate, pleated pieces, while the British maker Sarah Kelly wants her Saloukee paper jewellery collection to 'exude preciousness in the ordinary', elevating paper into more permanent form.

Another use of paper and paper pulp is in fashion design, with results ranging from the conceptual to the practical. Lynne Allen's moccasins (see p.139) reference paper's associations with memories and history – in particular the lost heritage of her Native American forebears. The Japanese fashion designer Issey Miyake – known for his innovative experiments with the likes of horsehair, foil and raffia – is inspired by the 'the culture of paper'. In the early 1980s, he reworked the Japanese tradition of Kozo-paper workwear using shapes from Western streetwear; he returned to it again in his Spring/Summer 2013 menswear collection. *Vogue* described how: 'In sporty outerwear or sharp tailoring, treated to be water-repellent, twisted to make yarn that was woven into canvas, or knitted into ikat-dyed pieces, washi [paper] proved itself startlingly versatile.' As Miyake so skilfully demonstrates, there are countless inspiring uses for paper as material.

Above: A papier-mâché figure beckons from
a window in La Boca neighbourhood, Buenos
Aires, Argentina

Left: Mask, 1972, Varanasi, India
Papier mâché, 29.5 x 30 cm (11½ x 12 in.)
V&A: IS.10-1977

PAPER MAKING

Rags make paper, 1987

In Europe until the mid-nineteenth century, when wood pulp was first used, paper was made from the fibres of used textiles, or rags. By the late 1700s, demand often exceeded supply, and rags became an increasingly valuable resource. This concertina book, made by Italy-based American visual artist Angela Lorenz, features an eighteenth-century saying that reflects the, then dual, perception of rags, paradoxically associated with both wealth and poverty:

Rags make paper, Paper makes money,
Money makes banks, Banks make loans,
Loans make beggars, Beggars make rags.

The book embodies these lines, as it consists of five paper leaves handmade from rags and paper money, and hinged with fabric strips. When closed, it is wrapped in a brown piece of fabric tied with string, like a beggar's bundle.

Angela Lorenz
Handmade rag paper, rags, paper money and hemp twine, USA,
25.4 x 20 cm (10 x 8 in.; closed), 25.4 x 91.4 cm (10 x 36 in.; extended)
National Art Library, V&A: 38041992100156

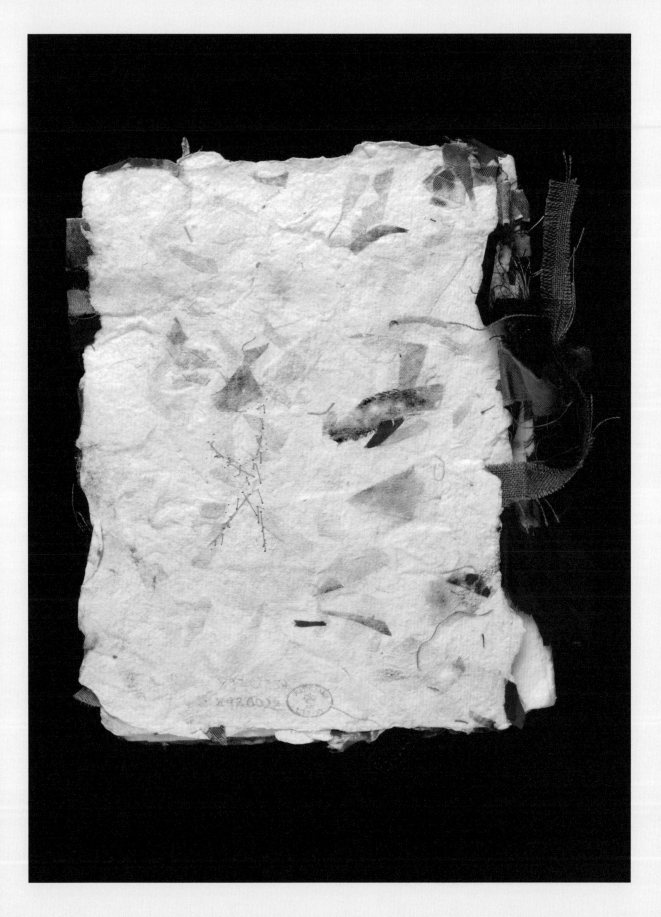

HANDMADE PAPER BOOKLET

This simply-folded and sewn booklet consists of blank paper pages contained by a decorative handmade cover. The basic raw ingredients are coloured papers and rose petals, with book pages or other manuscript paper used to enliven the cover with your own personal message. The paper-making process is a bit messy, but produces elegant results.

Project by Mandy Brannan

You will need

6 sheets A4 pastel-coloured lightweight copy paper, approx. 80 gsm
1 brightly-coloured disposable/paper napkin
2 uncoated textbook, or similar manuscript, pages, approx. 10 x 16 cm (4 x 5½ in.)
Cotton linter mesh, 10 x 10 cm (4 x 4 in.)
Containers/bowls for soaking paper
6 roses, petals separated and dried (alternatively, shop-bought, pre-dried petals)
Stainless steel or enamel saucepan
1 tbsp (⅟₁₆ cup) washing soda
Wooden spoon
Sieve
Blender
Simple mould and deckle, 14 x 20 cm (5½ x 8 in), shop-bought, or to make your own see below and p.134
Plastic container/washing-up bowl into which the mould and deckle will fit
2 small towels
2 pieces mid-weight interfacing, approx. 30 x 40 cm (12 x 16 in.)
2 flat boards, approx. 50 x 60 cm (20 x 23½ in.)
Tea-towel
Brick, or other comparable weight
Iron and ironing board
Cutting board
Craft scissors/knife with blades
Metal ruler
Bone folder
Awl
30 cm (12 in.) fine jute string
Tapestry needle

Optional (to make a mould and deckle)

Lengths of 2 x 2 cm (¾ x ¾ in.) wood: 4 x 24 cm (9½ in.) lengths 4 x 14 cm (5½ in.) lengths
Hammer and nails or wood glue
Fine netting, 18 x 24 cm (7 x 9½ in.)
Staple gun

How to make

Making a mould and deckle

A mould and deckle is available to buy ready-made from craft stores, but you can easily make your own. If you can find two identical picture frames, you can use those instead of making the frames. **Note:** *The interior measurement of your frame will be the size of your finished sheet of paper.*

1 Make two identical frames by hammering or gluing together the wooden lengths as shown at each corner.

2 Staple the fine netting in place to one of the frames, as shown, pulling the netting taut as you go. This frame will become the mould, on which the paper is formed. The other is the deckle, which creates straight edges on the paper sheet.

Deckle

Mould

Tear the papers into small pieces, starting with the pastel copy paper (below), then the napkin, book pages and linter.

Making the cover sheet

1 Tear three of the copy-paper sheets into postage-stamp-sized pieces, place in a container and cover with water. Repeat with the paper napkin, book pages and cotton linter, each in a separate container. Leave to soak for 30 minutes.

2 While the papers are soaking, place the dried rose petals in a saucepan, cover with cold water and add the measured washing soda. Stir with a wooden spoon, bring to the boil, reduce the heat and simmer for 15 minutes.

3 Take the pan off the heat and strain the rose petals through a sieve. Rinse the petals under cold running water until the water runs clear.

4 Fill the jug of your blender two-thirds full with cold water (approx. 1.4 litres/ 50 fl oz) and add a small handful of the torn copy papers. Blend on medium for 5 seconds, then high speed for 10 seconds, and then decant the pulped papers into a larger plastic container (a washing-up bowl is ideal).

5 Repeat step 4 with all of the remaining torn-up paper (the book pages, napkin and cotton linter), and add to the previous mix in the washing-up bowl, swirling with your hand until the desired mix of colours is created.

6 Add the rose petals to the mix. At this point, your washing-up bowl should be two-thirds full with water and pulped papers.

7 Dampen one of the pieces of interfacing. Fold one of the towels in half, place it next to your bowl and lay the dampened interfacing directly on top – this is your couching area.

8 Holding the mould and deckle with both hands (the mesh should be in the middle, sandwiched between the two frames, with the deckle on top), lower it into the water/pulp mix and scoop up a layer of pulp. Rocking the mould and deckle gently will allow the paper fibres to interweave and settle on the mesh evenly.

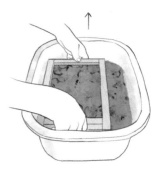

9 Hold the mould and deckle flat, above the bowl, allowing it to drain for 15 seconds. Lift off the top frame (deckle), turn the lower frame (mould) over and press it down on the interfacing.

10 Lift the mould away, leaving the pulp sheet on the couching area.

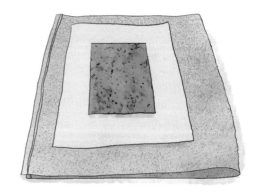

11 Cover the sheet with another piece of dampened interfacing and a second folded towel and press between boards for 10 minutes. Place a brick or other similar weight on top of the boards for extra pressure.

12 Uncover and carefully lift the newly formed sheet. Place it between the two layers of a folded tea-towel, and take it to your ironing board. With the iron on a medium heat, press the paper through the tea-towel until completely dry and flat. Place the sheet between heavy books until ready to use.

13 Place your finished sheet of cover paper on a cutting mat and trim the top and bottom level using a craft knife and metal ruler. Fold in half widthwise and press along the fold using your bone folder.

14 Open the cover sheet out and use a ruler and awl to make a hole/sewing point halfway along the fold. Make two more holes on the fold, 2.5 cm (1 in.) either side of the central hole.

Making up the book

1 Trim the three remaining copy-paper sheets – these will form the interior pages of your booklet – so that they are just a little smaller on all sides than the open cover sheet (see photograph on p.133). Fold each sheet in half, using the bone folder to neaten the fold.

2 Pierce the inner sheets with the awl in the same way as you did the cover sheet: once in the middle of the fold and again 2.5 cm (1 in.) each side of this point.

3 Place the folded sheets inside the folded cover sheet, lining up the holes.

4 Thread your tapestry needle with jute string. Holding all the sheets together, sew through the middle hole (A) from the outside, leaving a 10 cm (4 in.) tail of thread. Now sew outwards through the top hole (B), back in to the book through the lower hole (C), and out through the middle (A) again.

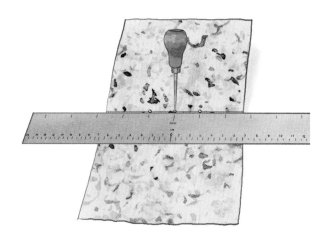

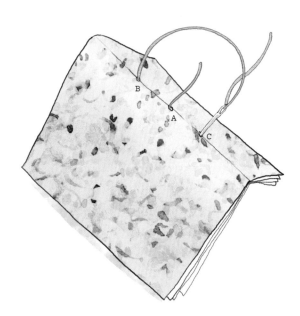

Trim the edges of your finished cover sheet using a craft knife.

5 Position the ends of the jute string so that they run either side of the long stitch on the outside of the fold. Now tie them together in a small bow and trim the ends.

6 Leave the finished booklet under some books or weights overnight to press.

Now try...

Individualizing your booklet. You can use unusual found papers and different flower petals to vary the effects achieved in your paper mix. You can also adapt the method to make a card or invitation rather than a booklet cover – rubber stamps work especially well to decorate this kind of paper.

STITCHED PAPER

Moccasins, c. 2000

Lynne Allen has Native American ancestry (she is descended from the Hunkpapa Sioux) and much of her work, connecting to this family history, has been inspired by the journals of Josephine Waggoner, her great grandmother. Moccasins are traditional Native American footwear, made of soft leather (often deerskin) decorated with embroidery or beading. Allen's moccasins (she has made several pairs) were cut and stitched from sheets of handmade cotton paper decorated with pulp paintings of animals, overlaid with etchings of text taken from the journals. Other text, printed from rubber stamps, is meaningless scribble, to suggest a lost history and lost culture. The finished moccasins were coated with shellac (a varnish) to protect the surface and to make them look aged and more like deer hide.

Lynne Allen
Etching, paper pulp and hand-painting on handmade paper, cut and stitched with linen thread, and lacquered with shellac, USA, 7 x 21 x 8 cm (2¾ x 8¼ x 3 in.)
V&A: E.3584:1-2–2004. Purchased through the Julie and Robert Breckman Print Fund

PAPER BAG

This bag – perfect as a gift, or for transporting light items (it's only really semi-functional, given the limited durability of paper) – is inspired by paper fashion and related artworks in the V&A collection. Instructions are given for four variations, pictured right. Paper is treated as if it were fabric, with machine-stitched seams. The basic bag has a fold-over flap, and the variations include a handle, a strap and buckle and a hand-stitched trim.

Project by Jennifer Collier

You will need

2-3 sheets A4 copy paper

Vintage/used map (min. A4 size required for the basic bag; A3 for the bag plus any of the variations)

HB pencil

Metal ruler or bone folder

Sewing pins

Sewing machine and threads, in white or colours to coordinate with your chosen map

Craft scissors

Craft knife

Glue stick, or PVA glue and applicator

Optional

Bag with strap and buckle: scrap of grey board, min. 5 x 5 cm (2 x 2 in.)

Bag with strap and buckle: hole punch

Bag with hand-stitched trim: 1 skein of thread, coton á broder or similar, in a colour to coordinate or contrast with your map

Bag with hand-stitched trim: Hand-sewing or embroidery needle

How to make

Basic bag

1 Photocopy or otherwise enlarge the
bag template 1 on p.146 using your chosen
method (see p.19 for full instructions).
Transfer the template to your map paper
by drawing round it with a pencil. Transfer
the dotted fold lines, then cut out.
Note: *Lay the template on your map 'upside
down' so that the map appears on the front
of the bag in the correct orientation.*

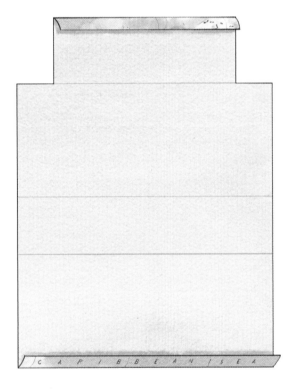

2 Fold the bag along the dotted lines,
towards the wrong side and using a ruler
or bone folder to achieve sharp folds.
Rub out any remaining visible pencil lines.
Fold the top and bottom hems of the bag
over to the wrong side and, using your
sewing machine, sew with a long running
stitch, on the outside, to give the bag
a neat finish and to strengthen it. Tie
off loose ends. **Tip:** *Practise on a piece
of scrap map paper first. Make sure you
are sewing, rather than cutting, the paper.
Be sure to tie off loose ends, not reverse
stitch as you might on fabric.*

3 With right sides together, line up the
top and bottom edges of the bag (excluding
the flap). Pin and stitch the two sides,
tying off the loose threads.

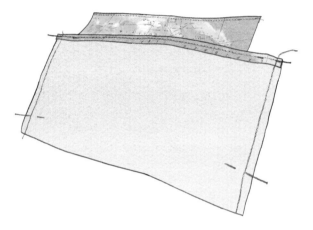

4 Keeping the bag wrong side out, push
one side seam down to line up with
the middle of the base of the bag (see
photograph opposite). Stitch across the
corner created, where a fold line appears.
Repeat at the same depth on the other side,
tie off and trim loose threads.

5 To soften the paper and prevent it
tearing when you turn the bag right side
out, scrunch the whole thing up! Ease it
flat again and, gently pushing from the
stitched bottom corners, turn the bag
right side out. **Tip:** *Take your time, as
this is the only point at which you really
risk tearing the paper.*

With bag wrong side out, stitch a line across each corner
as shown. This will create a flat base for your bag.

6   Fold a crisp vertical line from the
base (one end of your stitched line) to
the outside edge of the flap at the back
of the bag, on both sides. Repeat at the
front of the bag, from the base to the
top. Use a ruler if necessary to ensure
straight sides.

7   Push the stitched side edges of the
bag inwards to create a 'V' shape, and
fold over the flap to complete.

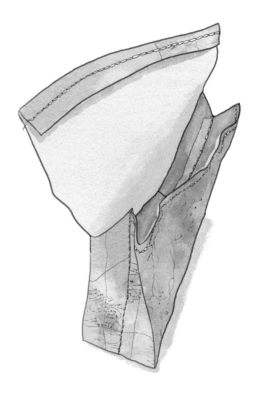

Bag with handle

1 Follow steps 1-7 for the basic bag.

2 Cut a strip of map paper measuring 30 x 6 cm (11¼ x 2⅜ in.). Draw a 1 cm (⅜ in.) hem along the length of the strip on both sides. Fold the hems inwards, to the wrong side, using a ruler or bone folder to get a crisp fold. Fold the entire thing in half again lengthwise, and pin to secure. Sew a line of long running stitches along the pinned edge.

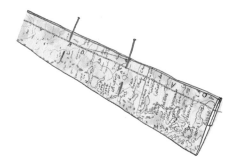

3 Fold a small (1 cm/⅜ in.) hem at each end of the handle, then pin the handle to the back of the bag, so that the hems are concealed. Position so that the handle edges line up with the creased sides of the bag.

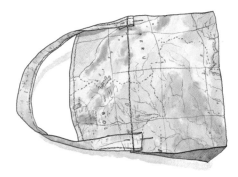

4 On the inside of the bag, sew a line of stitches across the width, approx. 0.5 cm (¼ in.) below the fold line of the flap, to secure the handle in place at both sides. Tie off the loose threads and trim.

Bag with strap and buckle

1 Follow steps 1-7 for the basic bag.

2 Photocopy or otherwise enlarge the strap template 2 on p.147 using your chosen method. Transfer the template to map paper as before.

3 Punch holes through the strap, as indicated by the template. You could also top-stitch around the outside of this piece, using contrasting thread, as a decorative detail (see photograph on p.141).

4 Trace the buckle templates 3 and 4 on p.147 and transfer to grey board — lay the templates on the board and draw over the lines with a pen, pressing hard, leaving an imprint to cut round. Cut out with scissors or a craft knife. With a dab of glue on the top, flat edge of piece 3 only, stick it in position on piece 4, following the illustration below. Do not glue the curved bottom edge of the prong down.

5 Push the buckle prong through hole A of the strap, so that it faces towards you, and down towards the body of the strap. Fold the short end of the strap over on the dashed line that runs through this hole. Stitch a line across the strap, 1 cm (⅜ in.) from the fold. Tie off and trim loose ends.

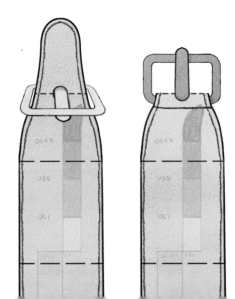

6 Now fold the strap again, in the same direction, along the three dotted lines, using a ruler to get a nice crisp fold in each case. The strap should now fit around the whole bag, the folds matching the contours of the bag, with the buckle end coming up from the base (see photograph on p.141).

7 Stitch the strap in place where it overlaps the top-stitching on the bag flap, so the two lines of stitching appear to have been done at the same time. Tie off the loose threads and trim them to the knot. **Tip:** *A dot of glue on the base of the bag will secure the strap in place here.*

8 Push the prong of the buckle through the hole on the strap to fasten the bag.

Bag with hand-stitched trim

1 Follow steps 1-7 for the basic bag.

2 Thread a hand-sewing needle with a 30 cm/12 in. length of thread and tie a knot at the end. Using the existing machine-stitched holes on the front of the bag flap, come through from the back of the first hole on the left, and then back down through the second hole, leaving a loop of thread. Running your needle through this loop, from back to front, pull the stitch tight to the edge of the flap, bringing the needle towards you, working a modified blanket stitch.

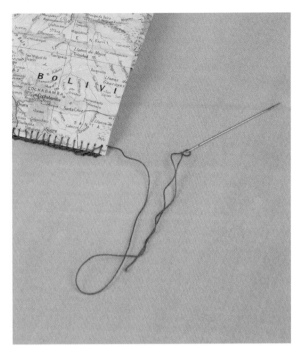

Pick out a colour from your map and match your thread to it, or use a contrasting colour.

3 Now take your needle back through the stitch you have just created along the edge of the flap, from front to back, making another thread loop – take the needle through this loop from back to front and pull this tight. Repeat three times, to bind the stitch, leaving the loop loose rather than tight, then one more time and pull tight to lock off the thread.

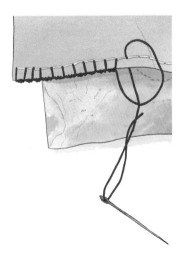

4 Repeat along the length of the flap, continuing to work in the existing machine-stitched holes. Tie off and trim loose ends.

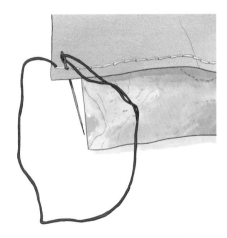

Templates

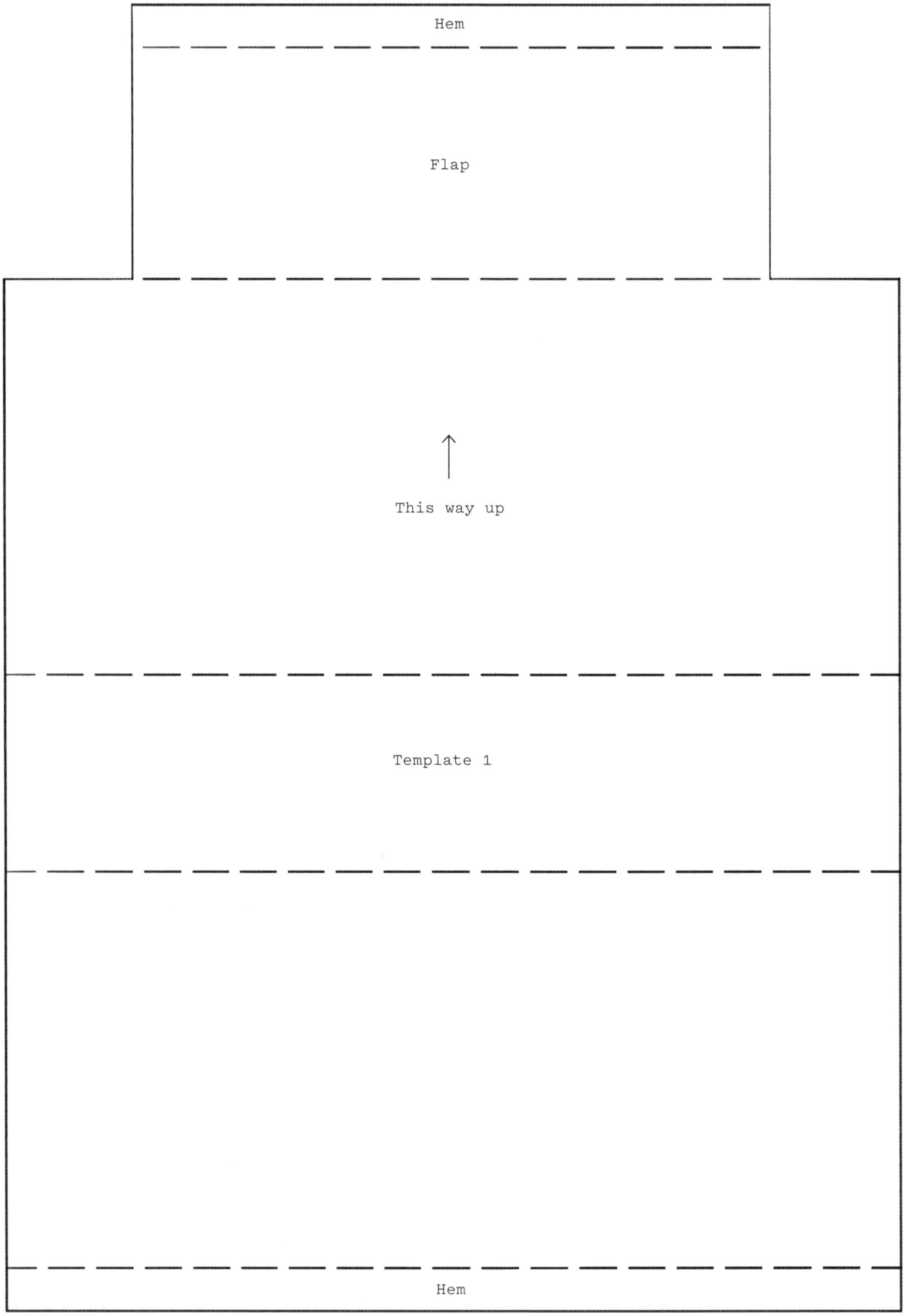

Hem

Flap

↑

This way up

Template 1

Hem

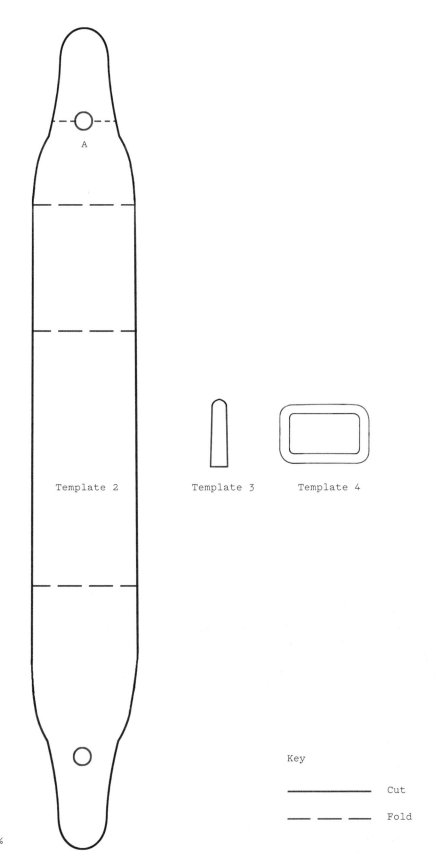

Template 2

Template 3

Template 4

A

Key

———————————— Cut

— — — — — Fold

Templates shown at 75%
(enlarge to 133%)

PAPIER MÂCHÉ

Painted and lacquered bowl, c. 1910

The creation of finely decorated papier mâché in the Kashmir region was once a specialized process divided into two stages. The first stage required the *sakhta-saz* (maker) to apply a layer of pulp made from a mixture of paper, cloth, straw and other ingredients to a mould. Once hardened and separated from the mould, it was covered with a coat of gypsum and glue, followed by a layer of small pieces of tissue paper to prevent cracking, after which the surface was rubbed and smoothed. In the second stage, the *naqash* (artist or pattern drawer), prepared the colours, applied gold leaf and then drew the pattern freehand on the object, carefully filling in the fine detailing before applying a final coat of varnish.

Papier mâché, painted and lacquered, Kashmir,
height: 16 cm (6¼ in.), diameter: 27 cm (10½ in.)
V&A: IS.1–1971

Playing cards and box, 19th century, Kashmir, papier mâché, painted and lacquered, 5.6 cm (2½ in.; diameter)
V&A: IS.1201-1883

PAPER PULP BOWL

This decorative paper pulp bowl takes inspiration from lightweight, papier-mâché household vessels such as those shown on pp.148–49, updated with a more rough and rustic modern finish. Recycled paper was used in our example, but you could also use bright-white copy paper or coloured papers, for a brighter end result. The paper pulp can be moulded using a plastic bowl, or used to cover a glass bowl, jar or vase if you prefer it to be waterproof.

Project by Debbie Wijskamp

You will need

Old newspaper, approx. 65 grams (2¼ oz)
2 large plastic bowls
2 litres (67 fl oz) boiling water
Electric stick blender (a food processor will not work as well)
Large towels
Approx. 100 ml (3 fl oz) PVA glue
Rubber or disposable gloves
Plastic bowl of your choice, to use as a mould, approx. 10-15 cm (4-6 in.) diameter, or glass bowl, jar or vase (for waterproof version)
Petroleum jelly

Optional

Strong craft scissors
Sandpaper, 240 or 400 grit size

How to make

1 Tear the old newspaper into small pieces (approx. 2 cm/¾ in.) and place these in a large plastic bowl.

2 Add approx. 2 litres (67 fl oz) boiling water to the bowl and leave to soak for at least 15 minutes.

3 Using a stick blender, blitz the paper-and-water mix to a smooth consistency.

4 Strain your mix over another plastic bowl, using an old towel as a sieve: lay the towel in the second bowl and pour the pulp in, then lift the towel to drain out the water.

5 Holding the towel over a sink, or outside, wrap it up, and twist or squeeze the towel until no more water will come out. You may need to finish off the process by hand, squeezing lumps of pulp to get the last drops of water out.

6 Transfer the paper pulp into a clean bowl and rub to a fine consistency with your fingers, so it resembles fine gravel.

Soak small scraps of newspaper in water before blending and straining.

7 Add the PVA glue and combine with the pulp, by hand, to achieve a soft, smooth dough (you may need to add a little extra glue, depending on the paper you are using). **Tip:** *You will probably want to wear disposable or old rubber gloves for this.*

8 If you are using a plastic mould, turn it over (onto a protected surface), and smear the outside with a layer of petroleum jelly. This will stop the bowl sticking to the paper pulp.

9 Now begin to mould your paper pulp dough over the bowl, working from the base to the lip and making sure the dough is pressed quite firmly onto the surface. You should try to achieve a layer of paper pulp approximately 3 mm (⅛ in.) thick.

10 To make a waterproof version, press the paper pulp directly onto your glass vessel, without applying petroleum jelly.

11 Leave to dry for at least 24 hours (depending on the temperature and humidity of the room), until solid, before gently easing the paper pulp away from the mould (if using). For the waterproof version, the glass vessel remains in place as part of the finished bowl.

12 You can leave your finished bowl as is, or cut away the rough top edges with strong scissors. If you prefer a smoother finish, use sandpaper on these edges.

Now try...

A little extra decoration. While the pulp on your mould is still moist, press flowers or prettily shaped leaves gently into the surface to give it some extra decoration. Once the pulp is dry, the flowers will stay in place on the surface.

PAPER FLOWERS

Doll in framed tableau, 1851 ⎯⎯⎯⎯⎯⎯⎯⎯⎯

The unknown maker of this piece assembled an intricate tableau of paper flowers as a setting for a miniature doll. The flowers in the backdrop are suspended on wires to give a three-dimensional effect. The tableau was created by hand in England in 1851, the date shown just above the doll's head, while the doll itself was mass-produced in Germany in the 1840s. The piece incorporates glass paper and a variety of coloured papers, including some with gold and silver metallic finishes, which were not widely available before the nineteenth century. The expansion of industrial paper manufacture at this time made amateur paper crafts of all kinds increasingly popular in Victorian England. The tableau was given by the artist Claud Lovat Fraser to his wife, actress Grace Inez Crawford, and later gifted to the V&A.

Wax over composition, cloth, kid, glass, mohair, wood, paper, Germany (doll), Great Britain (paper flowers), 30 x 24.25 x 8.25 cm (12 x 9½ x 3¼ in.; framed), V&A: MISC.465-1978

FRAMED CREPE-PAPER ANEMONES

Using traditional crepe-paper flower-making techniques, you can choose to make either individual flowers with stems to place in a vase, or a replica of this framed set of flower heads. Patience and dexterity are required, but once you've mastered the basic technique, almost any flower shape is possible!

Project by Susan Beech (A Petal Unfolds)

You will need

0.5-1 cm (¼-¾ in.) polystyrene balls or white plastic beads
18-gauge floral wire
Glue gun and glue sticks
Craft scissors
Light-green mid-weight (40-60 gsm) crepe paper, approx. 50 x 20 cm (20 x 8 in.)
PVA glue
White heavyweight (180 gsm) crepe paper, approx. 50 x 20 cm (20 x 8 in.)
Yellow marker or felt-tip pen
1 sheet A5 card, 300 gsm, for templates
Tracing paper
Pencil
Double-sided crepe paper in lilac, purple, magenta and white, approx. 25 x 50 cm (8 x 20 in.) in each colour
Wire-cutters

To make individual flowers

Brown mid-weight (40-60 gsm) crepe paper
Green heavyweight (180 gsm) crepe paper

To make a framed piece

Deep picture frame – we've used a 20 x 20 cm/8 x 8 in. frame
White card for backing the frame

Optional

Light green and mid/dark purple soft pastels and soft paint brush

How to make

1 Using a glue gun, attach a polystyrene ball or plastic bead to the top of a piece of floral wire, taking care not to pierce the ball. Allow to dry.

2 Cut a 2 x 2 cm (¾ x ¾ in.) piece of light-green crepe, stretch (in the direction of the grain, see p.13) between your fingers and then, using PVA glue (not the glue gun), stick this over the top of the polystyrene ball to cover, twisting and securing any excess paper underneath with glue. Set aside and allow to dry.

3 Cut a 1.5 x 11 cm (⅝ x 4½ in.) strip of white heavyweight (180 gsm) crepe paper against the grain. Stretch between your fingers until the wrinkles have smoothed out of the paper. Fold in half widthwise once, then again (so that the strip ends up a quarter of its unfolded length), and finely fringe the strip to half its width, using your scissors and following the grain of the paper. The finer you fringe, the better the flower will look. Colour the tips of the fringe with a yellow marker.

4 Twist or roll the fringing gently between your thumb and forefinger, while securing it with the other hand, to give the fronds texture. Dot some PVA glue on the lower-left, unfringed corner of the fringing strip and begin to wrap it round the green centre, aligning so that the bottom of the fringing comes halfway down the polystyrene ball/bead. Continue to wrap, adding glue to the bottom of the strip as you go, and secure the end.

5 Trace the templates on p.161 and transfer them to thick card (see p.19 for full instructions) before carefully cutting out each one. Using your templates, cut the petals from the crepe paper. For flowers 1 and 2, cut three of the larger petals and three of the smaller for each flower. For flower 3, cut ten petals using the template provided. **Note:** *Observe the grain lines marked with arrows on the templates – the paper grain should run the length of each petal. To fill a frame, as shown on p.157, you will need approximately 20 flowers: 8 of type 1, 7 of type 2 and 5 of type 3.*

6 Gently shape the petals, taking each one between your fingers and stretching the centre of each petal over the pads of your thumbs.

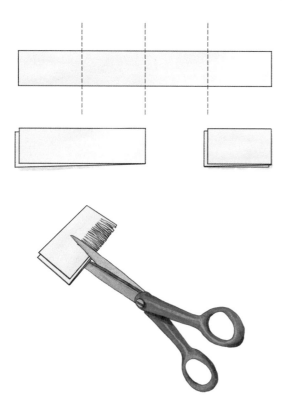

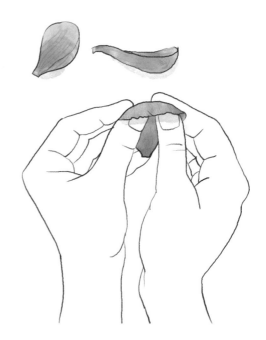

Make the centre of your flower and the stamen before adding crepe-paper petals.

7 Take a pair of scissors and gently scrape the edge of the closed blades over the back of each petal, on the top left and right edges, to curl them outwards slightly.

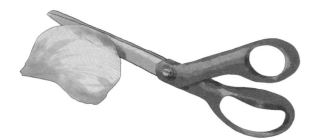

8 Take a prepared flower centre and separate out the petals needed to decorate it. Apply a small amount of glue to the bottom of each petal and secure to the flower head, just below the base of the fringing. For flowers 1 and 2, position the three largest petals first, at even intervals around the head, then fill the gaps with the smaller petals. For flower 3, place petals around the centre at 0.5 cm (¼ in.) intervals, then fill gaps with the remaining petals.

9 If you are making a framed piece, jump to step 13. Otherwise, to make a full-stem flower, trim the stem to your chosen length, using wire-cutters. To cover, cut a strip of brown crepe paper 1 x 15 cm (½ x 6 in.), against the grain, and stretch between your fingers until it is smooth.

Gently bend the stems of your finished flowers,
before displaying them in a vase.

10 Place a dot of PVA glue on the end and
wrap this strip around the stem, starting
underneath the bottom of the flower head
and wrapping at a 45-degree angle. Rotate
the flower with one hand, bringing the
crepe-paper strip down to the bottom with
the other. Secure with glue here and there
as you go, cutting and gluing the end of
the strip down at the bottom.

11 To add foliage, cut a piece of green
heavyweight (180 gsm) paper measuring 2.5
x 5 cm (1 x 2 in.), with the grain running
the length of the paper. Stretch between
your fingers until smooth and cut out a
leaf using the template on p.161. Repeat
to create a second leaf. Wrap the stem of
the flower with a brown strip of paper
for a second time, this time stopping
at the point at which you wish to insert
a leaf. Place a little PVA glue on the
very bottom point of the leaf and fix
to the brown strip, bringing it round
and gluing the second leaf on the other
side of the flower. Carry on wrapping
the brown paper to the end of the stem.

12 Add further colour to your flowers,
if you like, by gently adding some soft
pastel around the centre. Use a soft
paint brush and a chalk-pastel shade
slightly darker than the paper you're
working with. Gradually build the colour
around the flower head, blending the
pastel out gently as you go.

13 To make the framed piece, use wire-cutters to cut the flower heads from the floral-wire stems, cutting flush with the bottom of the excess paper underneath the flower.

14 Cut a piece of white card to fit inside your frame, as a backing. Place inside the frame and also carefully remove any glass. Using the glue gun, apply a small amount of glue to the base of each flower and position on the card, holding firmly until each flower is secured. Keep adding flowers until you've covered the area inside the frame (you may need to make a few extras, depending on how tightly you pack the frame), overlapping the flowers and petals here and there. **Tip:** *You can fill in any small gaps with spare petals if needed.*

Now try...

Your own flower designs. You can trace the petal shapes from real flowers in order to replicate the appearance of daisies or gerberas, or almost any flower you like. Using fringing only, rather than a ball/bead flower head, at the centre of your flower, will also extend the range of species you can make in paper.

Design templates

Flower 1 (medium)

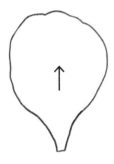 

Flower 2 (small)

Flower 3 (large)

Leaf

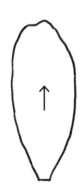 

↑ Grain direction

Templates shown at 100%

PAPER WEAVING

Three woven paper jars, 2009–12

Contemporary Korean artist Lee Young Soon created these handmade jars using the *jiseung* technique, an ancient method of weaving *hanji*, traditional Korean mulberry paper. *Jiseung* originates in the Joseon dynasty (1392–1910), when discarded *hanji* sheets used in calligraphy began to be recycled. These were shredded into thin strips that were then rubbed, twisted and tightly woven into daily objects such as lanterns, shoes, kitchenware and chamber pots. Some were coated with lacquer, perilla oil or persimmon juice to make them watertight. The inked part of the paper provided a speckled effect in the woven pieces, while white margins were reserved for luxurious items. *Jiseung* products were originally restricted to the upper class but their use spread to commoners towards the end of the dynasty, as books and *hanji* became more widely available.

Lee Young Soon
Hanji, *jiseung* technique, South Korea, height x widest point: 35 x 31 cm (13¾ x 12 in.); 32 x 24 cm (12½ x 9½ in.); 26 x 25 cm (10¼ x 10 in.)
V&A: FE.78-80-2015. Purchase funded by Samsung

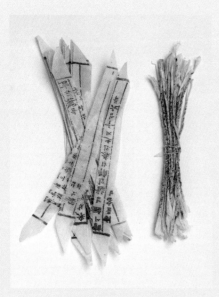

The woven paper jars were made by rubbing and twisting *hanji* as well as pages from recycled books.

WOVEN PAPER-YARN NECKLACE

Finger knitting is a technique believed to have been in use for centuries. This project was inspired by ancient Asian natural-fibre works created in paper using twisting, braiding, knitting and knotting techniques. Made using natural, environmentally friendly materials, this paper necklace is an accessible project for beginners but also offers a starting point for your own creative experiments.

Project by Sarah Kelly

You will need

28 m (90 ft) pastel-coloured paper yarn (we have used Rico Creative Paper 013)

Tape measure

Craft scissors

How to make

1   Measure out six lengths of paper yarn, each one 4.5 metres (14¾ ft). Take all six lengths and gather them together, so that one set of ends matches up. Wrap these into a loose coil to avoid any knots forming while you are weaving.

2   Measure 50 cm (19½ in.) from the loose ends of the yarn and pinch this point between your left-hand thumb and palm, with your palm facing towards you. The yarn tails should drop away from your hand and wrist, with the rest of the yarn tucked away behind your hand (this hidden bit is the length you will be working with).

3   Now tuck the yarn in front of the first finger and thread it between your first and middle fingers (you might want to hold the loose ends in place with your thumb). Wrap it around the back of the middle finger, bringing it completely around so that the cord comes back to the palm of your hand. Now wrap it back between your middle finger and behind the first, so that a cross is created between the two fingers. **Tip:** *Ensure that the tension of the weave is not too high by keeping your fingers spread at all times.*

4   Wrap the yarn back around your first finger until it is back in the palm, creating a figure of eight between the first and middle fingers.

Paper yarn

Paper yarn can be found in many craft stores and online. There is a huge range to choose from, including paper raffia, paper cord and paper twine, all of which have differing qualities. All variants will work for this project, giving a range of beautiful outcomes. We encourage you to explore the possibilities of the material and see what twists on this project you can invent.

Tip: *We have used six strands of yarn to create our necklace. It is possible, once you get the hang of the technique, to use more or fewer strands; you may also want to use a range of strand colours to create even more eye-catching necklaces.*

5 Now repeat steps 3 and 4, to create a second figure of eight above the first, then secure the tail of the working yarns between the thumb and first finger of your wrapped hand.

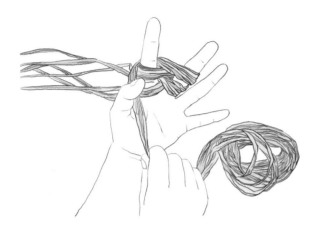

6 Using your free, non-wrapped hand, you can now start creating your necklace stitches. Starting with the middle finger of your wrapped hand, and working from the front of the hand to the back, take the yarns closest to the base of the finger, loop them up and over the yarns above and then up and over the top of the finger (you will need to bend the finger to allow this to happen). **Tip:** *Ensure that when looping your yarns up and over your finger, that you have got hold of all six of your yarns, to avoid loose and confused stitches.*

7 Repeat this action with your first finger, looping the yarns from the base up and over the next set of yarns and then over the top of your finger. This initial stitch will be a little loose, as it's the beginning of your necklace, so, once complete, give the tail a gentle tug to tighten the stitches. **Tip:** *When learning this technique, you will find that you need to make gentle adjustments with your free hand to continually pull the yarns on your fingers down towards your palm. The fingers holding the yarns should always remain in a wide 'V' shape, to enable you to work with ease.*

8 Take up your working yarn ends again, from between your thumb and first finger, and repeat steps 3 and 4 to create a figure of eight above the existing one still on your wrapped fingers. Repeat the 'looping over' from steps 6 and 7, always working from your middle finger first and with your palm facing you. You will start to notice your necklace stitches forming at the back of the wrapped hand. **Tip:** *To create regularity in the stitches, gently tug on them from behind the hand, often, as shown below. This will ensure that, as the necklace gets longer, the tension remains consistent.*

9 Continue to repeat the stitching until the tube of stitches you have created measures approx. 40 cm (15½ in.) in length, leaving just one set of yarns on both fingers. Carefully remove the yarns from your middle finger and loop them onto your first. **Note:** *Should you wish to undo your piece and perfect it, this is your last chance!*

10 With your free hand, make a new loop with the working yarns, close to the existing yarns on your first finger. Very carefully slide the existing yarns off your first finger and thread this loop through both sets.

11 Take the tail ends closest to this end of the necklace and thread through the new loop just created. Tug the tails until tight, thus tying off this end of the necklace.

Repeat the stitches until your necklace is the required length, then tie off by making a loop.

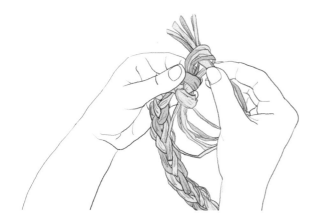

12 Use a finger to find the two end sets of yarn at the other end of the necklace and repeat the tying off process here.

13 Your necklace is almost finished – all that's left to do is to knot it to a length of your preference. Using a mirror, take a look to see where you like the necklace to sit on your neckline – our preference is to have the necklace at bib height, so that it's long enough to wear by putting over your head, rather than knotting and unknotting it with every wear. Loosely knot the ends of the yarns as symmetrically as possible.

14 Finally, neatly trim any excess paper yarn, ensuring both sides are symmetrical.

The paper yarn used for this necklace has varying colours.
Experiment with bolder shades or mix up the colours.

Now try...

**This same technique can be used to make
a decorative woven placemat** – 64 metres
(209 ft) of paper yarn would be needed for a
mat 20 cm (7⅞ in.) in diameter, made by coiling
a tube of stitches (made in the same way as the
necklace) round itself, with the working end of
the yarn threaded through each 'pass' of the
yarn, to hold the whole together. The Rico yarn is
perfectly suited to this technique – it is wide and
therefore conceals the structural threads.

Note: *These instructions have been written
from a right-handed maker's perspective.
Left-handers should still be able to
follow but, if you're finding it difficult
wrapping the yarns around your left hand,
you can always swap and apply the same
wrapping principles on your right.*

*The technique in general may take a
little practice to perfect but you can
unravel your attempts and start again up
to step 9 – just take the yarn off your
fingers and give the longest end a gentle
tug. The stitches should come free and you
can start again, as many times as you like.*

ABOUT THE MAKERS

Susan Beech

Based in Brighton, UK, Susan Beech is founder of A Petal Unfolds, specializing in the making of crepe-paper flowers, where each piece of paper is meticulously hand cut and shaped. Originally trained in Fine Art at the University of Brighton, she began working solely with paper in 2013. Susan has worked with clients including Liberty, Tatty Devine and kikki.k. She also teaches paper flower making and holds regular workshops in London.
www.apetalunfolds.com
[instagram] @apetalunfolds
[facebook] A Petal Unfolds

Mandy Brannan

Mandy Brannan is a London-based paper maker, book artist and workshop leader. While living in California during the 90s Mandy studied Japanese and Western styles of paper making, which led to the development of a personal style that involves experimenting with different fibres, plant materials and pigmentation methods. She uses complex layers of the paper making fibres that are manipulated into patterns influenced by her research into architectural details. #mjbooks
www.mandybrannan.co.uk
paperpypr.blogspot.co.uk
[facebook] Mandy Brannan Papermaker & Book Artist

Clare Bryan

Clare Bryan's work involves the manipulation and cutting of paper, making scalpel drawings in what first appear to be blank book structures. She combines teaching at various London colleges with small-press work and often collaborates with other artists, on artists' books and boxes. She has exhibited throughout the UK, with work in various public and private collections, including the Yale Centre for British Art, the Government Art Collection and the Tate.
https://cargocollective.com/clarebryan

Jennifer Collier

Paper pioneer Jennifer Collier creates sculptures from recycled materials in conjunction with stitch; a contemporary twist on traditional textiles. Through this marriage of unlikely materials old papers are transformed into something truly unique, delicate and complex. Jennifer completed a BA (hons) in Textiles in 1999 at Manchester Metropolitan University, is internationally exhibited, and has had her work featured in over sixty magazines and over fifteen books to date.
www.jennifercollier.co.uk
[instagram] [twitter] @paperjennifer
[facebook] Jennifer Collier 77

Sarah Kelly

Sarah Kelly set up her jewellery brand Saloukee in 2008, and since then has been making items that she describes as unusually unconventional, elegantly oversized and brilliantly British. Her collections have received international press coverage and have been sold worldwide, as well as being seen in retailers such as the National Portrait Gallery, Somerset House and Anthropologie. Sarah is also a published author and university lecturer.
www.saloukee.com
[instagram] [twitter] [pinterest] @saloukee
[facebook] saloukeejewellery

Roma McLaughlin

Roma McLaughlin currently lives and works in Melbourne. She has previously worked as a freelance illustrator on books for both adults and children, and has taught drawing and painting to all age groups. More recently Roma has developed an interest in the art of papercutting. This medium has allowed her to explore the intricacies of patterning, contoured shapes and silhouetting, which she uses in her images of everyday life. Currently she holds papercutting workshops and exhibits her papercuts in solo shows and group exhibitions in Australia and internationally.
www.romamclaughlin.com
[instagram] @romamcl
[facebook] Roma McLaughlin (Artist)

Ankon Mitra

Ankon Mitra is a pioneer of origami and folding techniques in architecture and design. He has taken paper folding techniques to metal, leather, wood, polypropylene, ceramics and concrete. He has shown his art at solo shows and group shows in India and the UK. He has taught at colleges of architecture, engineering and design in India and Singapore. He is a member of the British Origami Society and Origami USA. Speaking at the TEDx Conference in Delhi in 2015, he exhorted that the Universe is made and unmade from folding and unfolding. He is working towards creating an Origami University dedicated to the study and research of folding techniques for all disciplines. Since 2010, Ankon has conducted over fifty workshops on origami and its multifarious applications.
[facebook] Oritecture
[instagram] @ankonmitra

Clare Pentlow

Clare Pentlow combines precision hand-cutting, folding and layering to create mesmeric pieces of art that have a hypnotic sense of depth, drawing the viewer in. The drive for perfection constantly pushes Clare to cut ever smaller, using more layers and increasing the sense of movement in her work. She exhibits her work throughout the UK, running workshops to promote the simplicity and the complexity of working with paper. She has undertaken commissions for companies including Hermès.

www.cjpdesigns.co.uk
 @cjpdesigns

Samantha Quinn

Samantha Quinn is a freelance graphic designer and paper artist based in London. She has experience working with private and commercial clients on paper commissions and has worked with brands including Fossil, Converse and Victoria's Secret. Samantha heads up the Paper Artist Collective with fellow paper artist Kristine Braanen (www.paperartistcollective.com), an international community of paper artists founded in 2015 that brings together like-minded creatives with a shared love of paper. The group has over eighty members from twenty-six countries and has exhibited around the world.

www.squinnandco.co.uk
@squinnandco
f squinnandco

Sena Runa

Sena Runa began quilling in 2012 while she was searching online for inspiration for a new hobby. After three years, she decided to leave her corporate job for good and started a new chapter in her life. In 2015, she was chosen as a Selected Artist in a 20th Century Fox sponsored competition in association with *The Peanuts Movie*. Her work has featured in print and online publications including My Modern Met, Flow Magazine, Colossal, Bored Panda and 9 Gag. She is the author of *Quilling Art*.

www.senaruna.com
@senaruna
f senaspaperquilling
E senaruna

Julianna Szabo

Julianna Szabo is a London-based creator of intricate, hand-cut paper sets and illustrations. In her work, she likes to elevate a sheet of paper to the 3rd dimension and often brings it to life through stop-motion animation, using visual metaphors to draw you into a tactile world. She also has a passion for typography, which grew out of her graphic design education at the National College of Art and Design in Dublin, Ireland. Her main source of inspiration is her love of nature, but moving to a different country and experiencing different culture from that which she grew up in is also a great source of ideas.

www.juliannaszabo.com
 @juliannaszabo
f JuliannaSzaboIllustration

Florrie Thomas

Florrie is a London-based freelance artist specializing in paper illustrations. She fell into papercutting by accident in the final year of her Multi-Media Textile Degree, when her course leader saw a paper piece she was experimenting with and persuaded her to do her final show in paper. She hasn't stopped cutting since. Influences stem from antique lace, nature, folk art, print design, typography and nostalgia, which often entwine throughout her work. Her intricate style has lead to window displays, editorial features, papercut commissions, jewellery and also collaborations with other designers in this exciting medium. Recently she has been teaching papercutting workshops across London and Surrey.

www.papercutsbyflorrie.com
@florrie_ann

Samuel Tsang

Samuel Tsang is a London- and Amsterdam-based origami teacher, and the author of *The Book of Mindful Origami* and *The Magic of Mindful Origami*. He has folded origami since a child and has been teaching professionally since 2003. During that time he has introduced origami to thousands of students at corporate team-building events and public workshops. He runs an online origami florist (www.sesames.co.uk).

www.mindfulorigami.com
@mindfulorigami
@mindFOLDness

Debbie Wijskamp

Debbie Wijskamp designs and produces handmade interior products and objects, and collaborates with various companies and brands. Her work can be found in collections all over the world. She is inspired by everyday objects and materials, and much of her work is made from 'upcycled' materials, with a special interest in old or discarded paper. She runs courses from her own workshop, and gives guest lectures at art colleges.

www.debbiewijskamp.com
@debbiewijskamp
f debbiewijskamp

INDEX

Picture credits

8 above right: Courtesy Richard Sweeney
8 below: Courtesy Sikkema Jenkins & Co.,
New York. Photo Erma Estwick. © Kara Walker
9 above left: Courtesy Lydia Ricci
9 below left: © Meyersohn & Silverstein.
All rights reserved, DACS 2018
9 below right: Courtesy Chrissie Macdonald.
Photo John Short
20: Courtesy Jun Mitani
21 above: Fanometry, from the Street Fans
exhibition at www.thefanmuseum.org.uk.
Courtesy Annatomix (www.annatomix.com)
and Sylvain Le Guen (www.sylvainleguen.com).
Photo Rhian Cox
22: Library of Congress, Washington, DC
23: Rex/Shutterstock
24 above: Courtesy Cristian Marianciuc,
@icarus.mid.air
24 below: Mellimage/Dreamstime
33: Museum of Fine Arts, Boston
46 above: Courtesy Lisa Lloyd
47 above: John Mitchell/Alamy Stock Photo
48: Courtesy Bovey Lee
49 above: Krystyna Szulecka/Alamy Stock Photo
49 below: Courtesy Paper-Cut-Project
51 Courtesy: Swoon
63: The Horniman Museum and Gardens,
London
88 below: The Metropolitan Museum of Art,
New York
89 above: Courtesy Deniz & Türker Akman,
Paperatelier.com
90: Private Collection/Christie's Images/
Bridgeman Images
91: The Trustees of the British Museum, London
92 top: © Clifford Richards
93: Private Collection/Bridgeman Images
125 above: DeAgostini/G. Nimatallah/Diomedia
125 below: RSBPhoto/Alamy Stock Photo
129 above: Danita Delimont RM/Kymri Wilt/
Diomedia
130–31: ©Angela Lorenz
www.AngelaLorenzArtistsBooks.com
138–39: © Lynne Allen

Acknowledgments

The publishers would like to thank the V&A curators
who wrote historical texts, as follows: p.26 Janet
Birkett; p.52 Malcolm McNeill; p.70 Louise Cooling;
p.78 & p.130 Catherine Yvard; p.94 Leela Meinertas;
p.104 Melissa Lewis; p.110 Ursula Geisselmann; p.138
Gill Saunders; p.148 Divia Patel; p.162 Rosalie Kim.
Our thanks also go to Frances Ambler, who wrote
the chapter introductions, and Samantha Quinn,
for technical text and advice.

We would love to see what you create! Share your
pictures online using the hashtag #vamMaker